CAN YOU TAKE THE HEAT?

CAN YO
THE H

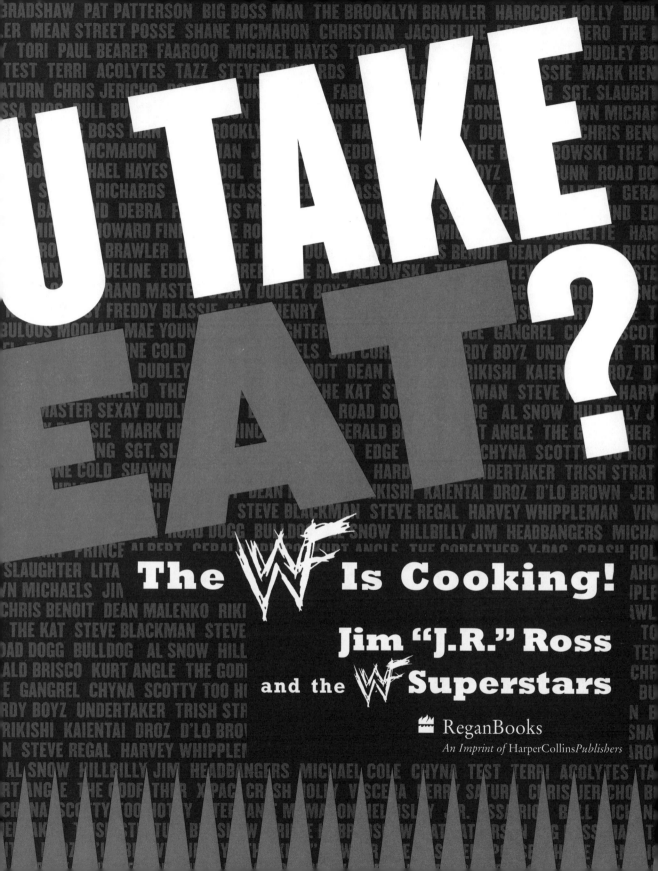

U TAKE EAT?

The WWF Is Cooking!

Jim "J.R." Ross and the WWF Superstars

ReganBooks
An Imprint of HarperCollinsPublishers

HarperCollins books may be purchased for educational, business, or sales
promotional use. For information please write: Special Markets Department,
HarperCollins Publishers Inc., 10 East 53rd Street, New York, NY 10022.

*Gangrel created by White Wolf Inc. Gangrel is a trademark of White Wolf Inc.
All rights reserved.

FIRST EDITION

Designed by Joel Avirom and Jason Snyder
Design assistant: Meghan Day Healey

Printed on acid-free paper

Library of Congress Cataloging-in-Publication Data
Ross, Jim, 1952–
    Can you take the heat? : the WWF is cooking / with Jim "J. R." Ross.—1st ed.
        p. cm.
    ISBN 0-06-039378-5
    1. Cookery, American. 2. World Wrestling Federation. I. Title.
    TX715.R8375 2000
    641.5973—dc21   00-062839

00 01 02 03 04 ❖/RRD 10 9 8 7 6 5 4 3 2 1

CONTENTS

LEAN AND MEAN: Lighter Fare—Just as Fun, with Less Fat

TAG-TEAM CLASSICS: Side Dishes and Breads

FINISHING MANEUVERS: Desserts

VICTORY CELEBRATION: Beverages

ACKNOWLEDGMENTS

Two of my greatest loves are eating good food and talking about my experiences with the talented men and women of the World Wrestling Federation, and *Can You Take the Heat?* more than fills the bill on both fronts! In this cookbook, you will enjoy a wide variety of delicious recipes from all the Superstars (even a few recipes that have been in my family for generations) and will get an up-close, behind-the-scenes look at the most talented sports entertainers in the world. Good groceries and the World Wrestling Federation: an unbeatable tag team!

Jim Ross

TONIGHT'S CARD: INTRODUCTION

THE OPENING Appetizers and S

G MATCH:

s, Salads,

oups

SGT. SLAUGHTER'S MESS HALL DIP

"**To his longtime pals,** Sarge is known as much for his Mess Hall Dip as he is for his prominent chin. Sarge and I used to share a room (with two beds, I should add) in the 'luxurious' Belmont Motor Inn in Baton Rouge, Louisiana, early in our careers. The hotel was cheap, eight dollars a night, which we split, and right down the street from a little Chinese restaurant the wrestlers frequented a couple days a week. He introduced me to Sweet and Sour Chicken, and after a sake or two, Sarge could damn near balance an entire egg roll on his chin!"

4 tablespoons (½ stick) garlic butter

2½ to 3 pounds ground sirloin

Salt to taste

Pepper to taste

3 (10.5-ounce) cans Hormel (or equivalent) no-bean chili

2 (8-ounce) packages cream cheese (or reduced-fat cream cheese)

3 cups (12 ounces) shredded mild cheddar cheese

12 ounces sour cream, or more if desired

Black olives (optional)

At-ten hut!! Okay, at ease and listen up!!

1 In a large frying pan, melt the garlic butter over medium-low heat. Add the ground sirloin and brown it thoroughly, adding salt and pepper to your liking. Take the pan off the heat and drain the grease from it, then put it back on the stove and drop down and give me twenty!

2 Now snap back up to your feet and stir the chili into the ground sirloin over medium heat. Add the cream cheese and stir. Have I made myself clear? Good, then carry on! Add the shredded cheese to the sirloin mixture, stirring until melted. (If the cheeses aren't melting fast enough, turn up the heat, maggot, but keep stirring so that it doesn't scorch.)

3 While you're waiting for everything to cook, ask yourself, "Have I ever dug a foxhole?" . . . Good, how deep? When all the cheese is melted, empty the mixture into a large bowl and smooth it with a spoon. Let it set for 10 to 12 minutes so that the top of the dip hardens.

4 Spread the sour cream (after 10 to 12 minutes, remember?) over the top of the dip with a spoon. You can decorate the sour cream with black olives—I usually spell out "Mess Hall Dip" on mine.

5 Serve with tortilla chips or corn chips. I like to use round white corn chips (not too salty).

Enjoy, and that's an order! I have a secret recipe for Slaughter Steak too, but if I gave that out I'd have to use the Slaughter Cannon and the Cobra Clutch on you . . . I'll let you live with the Mess Hall Dip!

Any questions? Good—you are dismissed! See you at the obstacle course. At ease!

Serves a platoon!

THE SARGE drew from his military background for this recipe, a good way to kick off any mission you and your troops embark on!

LITA'S MEXICAN-STYLE CEVICHE

"**Having trained** with the Hispanic male performers in Mexico City to launch her career, Miss Lita knows her Mexican-style dishes. She's quite the dish herself, especially if you like her dandy shoulder tattoo, which has no culinary significance whatsoever."

1¼ pounds fresh scallops, cut into bite-size pieces

¾ cup freshly squeezed lime juice (from 5 to 6 limes)

3 to 4 green chili peppers, peeled and chopped

½ cup chopped red onion

3 medium fresh tomatoes, peeled and cut into wedges

½ teaspoon coarse sea salt

Pinch of oregano

3 tablespoons olive oil

⅓ cup chopped cilantro

4 leaves iceberg lettuce

1 avocado, peeled, pitted, and sliced into wedges

1 Place the scallops into a wide, shallow, glass casserole, and pour the lime juice evenly over them. Cover and place in the refrigerator for 2 hours, stirring occasionally.

2 Add the rest of the ingredients, except the lettuce and avocado, and marinate for another hour, stirring occasionally.

3 Line 4 chilled wineglasses with the lettuce leaves, then top with the ceviche. Garnish with avocado wedges. Or serve on tortillas or with crackers.

Makes 4 servings

MICK FOLEY'S KNUCKLE SANDWICHES

"**Mick Foley certainly knows** how to use his knuckles, and as for the ham in this recipe, young Mickey was always a ham in class and in the locker room—not to mention in the ring. I wonder if the snipped parsley is a Foley family favorite or just something Mick thought up on his own? And remember, cutting these babies into quarters diagonally is strictly optional—and prohibited in Oklahoma!"

1 (4½-ounce) can deviled ham
¼ cup finely chopped celery
¼ cup finely chopped dill pickle
1 tablespoon low-fat mayonnaise
   or salad dressing
4 slices firm-textured white bread
4 slices firm-textured rye bread
1 (4-ounce) container whipped
   cream cheese (or reduced-
   fat cream cheese)
Snipped parsley or pimiento strips
   for garnish

1 In a medium bowl, combine the deviled ham, celery, dill pickle, and mayonnaise. Cover and chill.

2 Remove the crusts from the bread. Spread the slices of white bread with the ham mixture and top with the slices of rye bread. Frost the tops with cream cheese.

3 Cut each sandwich into quarters diagonally. Decorate the sandwiches with parsley or pimiento.

Makes 16 sandwiches

EDGE'S COCKTAIL PARTY MEATBALLS

"**He's young, he's Canadian,** he has wonderful teeth (all real), and he's a World Wrestling Federation Superstar! I was a little surprised about the grape jelly ingredient, but it sure tastes good. Just don't tell any of the macho men that there's jelly in the meatballs and you should be okay."

2 pounds lean ground beef

¼ cup peeled and grated potato

1 egg

1 small onion, grated

Salt to taste

Ground pepper to taste

1 teaspoon chopped parsley

1 (13-ounce) bottle chili sauce

3½ tablespoons (5 ounces) grape jelly

Dash of Worcestershire sauce

1 Combine the ground beef, potato, egg, and onion in a large bowl and mix well. Season the mixture with salt and pepper, then form it into small meatballs. Set aside.

2 In a large skillet, blend the remaining ingredients over medium heat. Add the meatballs, then cover and simmer about 30 minutes, stirring occasionally.

3 With a slotted spoon, transfer the meatballs to a chafing dish, fondue pot, or serving platter. Skim the excess fat from the sauce, then pour the sauce over the meatballs. Serve warm from the chafing dish.

Makes about 40 meatballs

"Don't be misled by the black nail polish, the Gothic attire, or the vampire look of Gangrel. He's not a bad guy, and there's nothing evil about his deviled eggs! When my dad would send me to the barn to gather eggs (hen fruit, he used to call them), I would always insist that Mom whip up some deviled eggs. I once ate twelve of them at a sitting . . . and then was introduced to castor oil. My suggestion is that you call a halt after eleven of these delights."

6 hard-boiled eggs
¼ cup mayonnaise or salad dressing
1 teaspoon vinegar
1 teaspoon prepared mustard
⅛ teaspoon salt
Paprika or parsley for garnish
    (optional)

1 Halve the hard-boiled eggs lengthwise. Remove the yolks and set the egg whites aside.

2 Mash the yolks with a fork, and stir in the mayonnaise, vinegar, mustard, and salt.

3 Stuff the egg whites with the yolk mixture and garnish with paprika or parsley, if desired.

Makes 12 servings

GANGREL'S DEVILED EGGS

DAVE AND EARL HEBNER'S CRAB-ARTICHOKE SPREAD

"**For ornery little twin brothers** who grew up in Virginia, Dave and Earl Hebner have become two of the Federation's most valuable resources. Earl is the senior referee in the Federation, while Dave serves as a road agent. Double trouble, so to speak—and this Hebner favorite is doubly good. The Hebners love the crabmeat-artichoke tag team, and so will you. Just as Earl and his minutes-older brother, Dave, love a good party, a good party loves this spread!"

1 (6-ounce) can lump crabmeat, drained

⅓ cup plain nonfat yogurt

⅓ cup mayonnaise

1 tablespoon lemon juice

1½ teaspoons cream-style horseradish sauce

1 teaspoon Worcestershire sauce

1 (14-ounce) can artichoke hearts, drained and coarsely chopped

Minced garlic to taste (optional)

1 Preheat the oven to 350 degrees.

2 In a large bowl, combine all the ingredients. Mix well.

3 Place in a 1-quart casserole. Bake at 350 degrees for 20 minutes, or cover with plastic wrap and microwave at 50 percent for 6 to 7 minutes, turning halfway through.

4 Serve warm with bagel chips or pita chips.

Makes 6 servings

CHYNA'S GUACAMOLE SALAD

"*Mama-cita!* How could you not like this one? Our ninth Wonder of the World is becoming a bona fide Hollywood celebrity—and Hugh Hefner's favorite World Wrestling Federation Superstar! This is a great dish to have on hand while watching *Raw* or *Smackdown,* but be sure to use fresh cilantro and don't skimp on the garlic!"

2 ripe avocados

2 teaspoons fresh lemon juice

¾ teaspoon salt

2 green onions, trimmed and thinly sliced

4 cherry tomatoes, chopped (optional)

½ teaspoon finely chopped fresh cilantro (optional)

1 clove garlic, peeled

4 cups mixed salad greens

1 Cut the avocados in half, remove the pits, and scoop out the flesh with a spoon. Combine with the lemon juice and salt in a bowl and mash.

2 Add the green onions to the mixture, and, if desired, the tomatoes and cilantro. Press the garlic through a garlic press and add it to the mixture. Chill in the freezer for 10 minutes.

3 Mound the greens on 2 large or 4 small plates, and top each with the guacamole.

Makes 2 to 4 servings

SCOTTY TOO HOTTY'S TOO COOL ORANGE SALAD

"From a teenage fan who used to write letters to the World Wrestling Federation (and even got answers) to a young wrestler with his own Jell-O recipe in this soon-to-be famous cookbook, this Portland, Maine, native has come a long way. What's next, a commercial with Bill Cosby?

"This summertime favorite of Scotty's is good any time of year, especially when you have a houseful watching *Raw Is War* on a Monday night!"

1 (3-ounce) package orange Jell-O

1 (12-ounce) container cottage cheese

1 (8- to 12-ounce) container Cool Whip

1 (8-ounce) can crushed pineapple, drained

2 cups mini marshmallows

1 Sprinkle the dry Jell-O over the cottage cheese. Add the Cool Whip, stirring gently. Add the pineapple and marshmallows and mix well.

2 Cover and refrigerate at least 4 hours before serving.

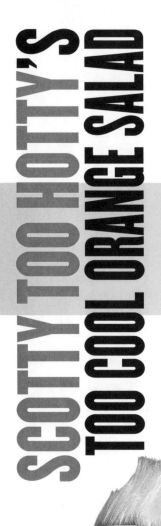

"TOO COOL" LOW-FAT TIPS:

✗ Use fat-free cottage cheese.

✗ Use sugar-free orange Jell-O.

✗ Use fat-free Cool Whip.

Makes 8 to 10 servings

STEPHANIE MCMAHON-HELMSLEY'S WALDORF SALAD

"**I'm not sure** how proficient lovely young Stephanie is in the kitchen, but if she's anything like her North Carolina–raised mother, she's probably a very good cook. This seems like one of those palate-pleasing dishes served only at fancy restaurants. I even refused to order it once years ago because it just sounded too froufrou—that is, until I had it during the holidays and discovered just how good it really was. This is a great dish for guys wishing to impress their significant others. In other words, anybody can make it! Nutritionists won't like this advice, but, for the best taste, don't use low-fat mayo. That's my story and I'm sticking to it!"

4 medium apples, cored and diced

1 tablespoon plus 1 teaspoon fresh lemon juice

½ cup chopped celery

½ cup halved seedless green grapes

½ cup chopped walnuts (or slivered almonds)

¼ cup raisins

½ cup mayonnaise or salad dressing

1 tablespoon sugar

½ cup whipping cream

Freshly ground nutmeg to taste

1 Add the apples to a large bowl, and sprinkle them with 1 tablespoon of the lemon juice. Add the celery, grapes, walnuts, and raisins.

2 In a small bowl, combine the mayonnaise, sugar, and 1 teaspoon of the lemon juice.

3 In another bowl, whip the cream until soft peaks form, then fold it into the mayonnaise mixture.

4 Spoon the mayonnaise mixture over the apple mixture and sprinkle the top lightly with nutmeg. Cover and chill.

Makes 8 to 10 servings

BLACK JACK LANZA'S
MANDARIN ORANGE AND RICE NOODLE SALAD

"'**Refreshingly marvelous**' is the only way to accurately describe this Lanza family favorite. Because it calls for only fresh ingredients, this super salad becomes a main event attraction just as the very respected Black Jack Lanza was in the squared circle for over two decades. Jack is now the senior road agent in the Federation and has been instrumental in the development of many Federation Superstars, including Stone Cold Steve Austin, who considers Jack his mentor. Black Jack Lanza is a legend in sports entertainment, and this dish will become a legend in your kitchen."

DRESSING:

- ¼ cup vegetable oil
- 1 tablespoon sugar
- 2 tablespoons white vinegar
- 1 tablespoon chopped fresh parsley

SALAD:

- ¼ head iceberg lettuce, torn into bite-size pieces
- ¼ head romaine lettuce, torn into bite-size pieces
- 1 cup sliced celery
- 2 tablespoons sliced green onions
- 1 (11-ounce) can mandarin oranges, drained
- 1 cup chow mein rice noodles

1 To make the dressing, in a medium bowl, whisk together the oil, sugar, vinegar, and parsley. Chill.

2 In a large bowl, mix the lettuces, celery, onions, and oranges.

3 Toss the salad and dressing to blend. Sprinkle the noodles on top.

Makes 4 servings

J.R.'S BAKED FRENCH ONION SOUP

"**Growing up in Westville,** Oklahoma, I never had French onion soup (most of Mama's soups had some kind of beans in them), but it became a room-service staple for me when I started traveling in the sports-entertainment business more than twenty years ago. As a matter of fact, for more than five years I had a bowl of French onion soup every Saturday night before broadcasting a Sunday Pay-Per-View show. Some sort of culinary superstition, I suppose. This recipe is one of my wife, Jan's, masterpieces."

4 tablespoons (½ stick) unsalted butter

4 large sweet onions (Vidalia are best), halved and thinly sliced

¼ cup sugar

Salt to taste

½ teaspoon coarse ground pepper

6 cups beef stock

2 tablespoons ruby port wine

4 large, thick slices French bread, toasted

1 cup grated Gruyère or Swiss cheese

1 Melt the butter in a large soup pot. Add the onions and wilt over medium-low heat, covered, for 20 minutes. Stir occasionally.

2 Sprinkle the sugar over the onions. Toss and cook, uncovered, until caramelized, about 10 minutes. Sprinkle with the salt and pepper.

3 Add 3 cups of the stock and simmer, uncovered, over medium heat for 15 minutes. Add the remaining 3 cups of stock and the port. Cook for another 30 to 40 minutes.

4 Preheat the broiler. Divide the soup among 4 ovenproof soup bowls. Top each bowl with a slice of toasted French bread and sprinkle the cheese evenly on top. Place the bowls under the broiler until the cheese melts.

Makes 4 servings

ESSA RIOS'S
BLACK BEANS AND CHICKEN SOUP EL GRANDE

"Because of all the black beans in this recipe, I suggest you enjoy this dish only before partaking in outdoor activities. After eating, everyone go in the backyard and play Whiffle ball or badminton or something. (Just kidding.) A talented wrestler, Essa is working hard to become a Light Heavyweight star. And if he doesn't, Essa may need to perfect a few more recipes . . . "

8 ounces boneless chicken breast, cut into pieces

1 tablespoon olive oil

¼ cup chopped onion

2 garlic cloves, minced

1 teaspoon ground cumin

½ teaspoon salt

½ teaspoon chili powder

⅛ teaspoon ground red pepper

4 cups low-fat chicken broth

1 (15-ounce) can corn (undrained)

1 (14½-ounce) can Mexican stewed tomatoes (undrained)

1 (15-ounce) can black beans (drained)

1 Sauté the chicken in the olive oil over medium heat until it is cooked through, about 10 minutes. Add the onion, garlic, cumin, salt, chili powder, and red pepper, and cook 10 minutes more.

2 Transfer the mixture to a stockpot, and stir in the chicken broth, corn, tomatoes, and black beans. Bring to a boil, then reduce heat and let simmer for 15 minutes.

Makes 6 servings

"**The Fink came to work** for the Federation on April 1, 1980. He's the company's longest running hit, and he's rarely out sick. (Well, he has been known to miss work to mourn a New York Jets or Mets loss.) It must be the chicken soup! It's gotta be, because moms and grannies have been feeding sick young 'uns chicken soup since before Fink had a full head of hair."

HOWARD FINKEL'S HEALTHFUL CHICKEN SOUP

- 1 quart chicken broth
- 1 cup chopped onions
- 1 cup chopped celery
- 1½ cups slivered cooked chicken
- ¾ cup cooked brown rice
- 1 cup finely shredded cabbage
- 1 cup diced tomatoes
- ¼ cup chopped radishes
- ¼ cup chopped scallions
- 1 tablespoon chopped parsley
- ½ cup chopped green pepper
- ¼ cup chopped cilantro leaves
  (or ½ teaspoon dried thyme
  or 1 tablespoon fresh thyme)
- Salt to taste
- Pepper to taste

1 Bring the chicken broth to a boil, then reduce heat and simmer.

2 Add the onions and celery, and simmer a few more minutes. Add the chicken and rice, and let simmer again.

3 Now add the remaining ingredients and continue stirring and simmering for 3 to 4 minutes longer, until vegetables are piping hot but still crunchy.

Makes 3 to 4 servings

BULL BUCHANAN'S BEEFY BARLEY SOUP

"**Young Bull must've eaten** a bunch of red meat when he was a pup down in Georgia to become the 6-foot 8-inch 295-pounder he is today! Bull's mama named him Barry, but how could you seriously tangle with a guy named Barry? You couldn't, so now we have Bull and a great recipe for those with Bull-like appetites. This dish falls in the 'so good you can't sit still and eat it' category."

2½ pounds beef short ribs

2 tablespoons cooking oil

7 cups water

1 (16-ounce) can tomatoes, cut up, with the liquid

2 tablespoons instant beef bouillon granules

1 large onion, sliced

1½ teaspoons salt

1 teaspoon dried basil, crushed

½ teaspoon Worcestershire sauce

⅔ cup quick-cooking barley

2 cups sliced carrots

1 cup sliced celery

½ cup chopped green pepper

¼ cup chopped parsley

Salt to taste

Freshly ground black pepper to taste

1 In a large kettle or Dutch oven, brown the short ribs in hot oil over low heat for about 10 minutes. Drain the oil from the pan. Stir in the water, tomatoes, bouillon, onion, salt, basil, and Worcestershire sauce. Cover and simmer for 1½ hours.

2 Stir in the barley, carrots, celery, green pepper, and parsley. Cover again and simmer for 45 minutes.

3 Remove from heat, and when cool enough to handle, remove the ribs. Cut the meat from the bones and chop it coarsely. Discard the bones.

4 Skim any fat from the soup, then return the meat to the soup and heat thoroughly. Season with salt and pepper.

Makes 8 servings

MIDEON'S MINESTRONE SOUP

"**Dennis Knight (Mideon)** is one of the funniest and most likable people I've ever encountered in this crazy business. Dennis will never make the cover of *GQ* or *Muscle & Fitness,* but this soup will hit the spot, especially if you use fresh vegetables, not frozen."

½ cup chopped onions

1 clove garlic, minced

2 tablespoons butter

3 cups chicken or beef broth

1 cup sliced carrots

½ cup chopped green beans

1 medium zucchini, cut in half lengthwise and then sliced

¾ cup chopped celery tops

2 cups slivered green cabbage or Swiss chard

½ teaspoon dried oregano

½ teaspoon dried thyme

¾ cup mixture canned white kidney beans and lima beans, or fresh peas

1 cup chopped parsley

1 cup chopped tomato

½ teaspoon salt

2 tablespoons olive oil (optional)

1 Sauté the onions and garlic in butter until soft. Add the broth and bring the mixture to a boil over medium heat. Add the carrots and the green beans, then reduce the heat and simmer for 2 or 3 minutes.

2 Add the zucchini and the celery tops and simmer until the zucchini begins to soften. Add the cabbage, oregano, and thyme and simmer again until the cabbage begins to soften. Add the beans and allow them to warm. Add the parsley, tomato, and salt and let simmer another 2 minutes. Add the olive oil if desired, and serve.

Makes 4 to 6 servings

Variation: You can also add beef, lamb, turkey, or chicken to this soup, but be sure that the meat matches the flavor of the broth you have chosen. Use chicken broth if you add chicken or turkey, and beef broth if you add beef or lamb.

THE MAIN EVENT

Entrées

THE ROCK'S FAMOUS ROCK-BOTTOM PANCAKES

"The Rock really does like pancakes, and he eats plenty of them, usually very early in the morning (the carbs thing, you know). The fresh bananas make this recipe especially good. This is another main-event-level recipe that must be tried in the comfort and safety of your own home."

1 ¼ cups flour

2 tablespoons sugar

2 teaspoons baking powder

½ teaspoon salt

1 egg, beaten

1 cup milk

1 tablespoon cooking oil

2 bananas (optional)

1 In a large bowl, stir together the flour, sugar, baking powder, and salt.

2 In a separate bowl, combine the egg, milk, and oil. Add this all at once to the flour mixture, stirring until blended but still slightly lumpy.

3 For a standard-size pancake, pour about ¼ cup of the batter onto a hot, lightly greased griddle or a heavy skillet. For a dollar-sized pancake, use only about 1 tablespoon of batter.

4 Cook the pancakes until golden brown, flipping them over when they have a bubbly surface and slightly dry edges.

5 To make The Rock's *favorite* kind of pancakes, slice the bananas into ¼-inch slices and place them in between the layers of the pancakes.

Makes about six 6-inch pancakes or 30 dollar-sized pancakes

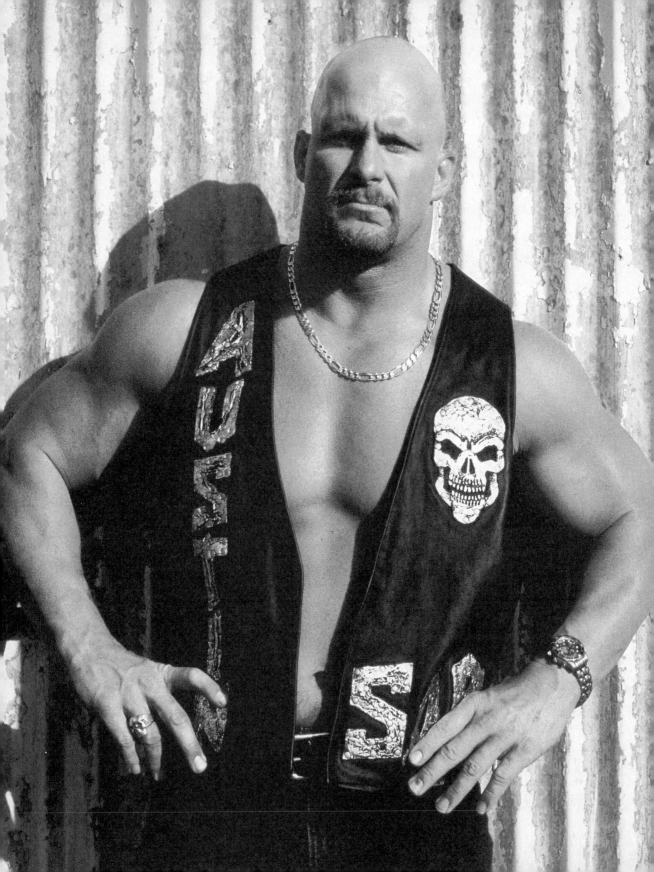

"Stone Cold is not a morning person, but this dish makes even the Texas rattlesnake smile at sunrise! Use large **brown** eggs and **Cinnabon** brand cinnamon, and then tell me you can sit still while eating this masterpiece!"

STONE COLD'S TEXAS TOAST

3 eggs

¼ teaspoon vanilla

½ cup milk

1 tablespoon sugar

¼ teaspoon ground cinnamon

Salt to taste

8 slices day-old, thick-sliced bread

Butter for frying

Pure maple syrup

1 In a shallow bowl, whisk together the eggs, vanilla, milk, sugar, and cinnamon, and add a dash of salt.

2 Dip the bread into the egg mixture, coating both sides.

3 Add a small amount of butter to a skillet and fry the bread on both sides over medium heat until golden brown. Serve warm with maple syrup.

Makes 4 servings

SHAWN MICHAELS'S SAN ANTONIO OMELET

"**Shawn Michaels was one** of the most gifted athletes I had ever seen. This high-strung Texan saw his career end much too soon due to a back injury, but his exploits as a World Wrestling Federation Champion will never be forgotten. This is a great dish that's especially good for dinner. It's very healthful, and you get to add personality with the Tabasco!"

¼ cup chopped yellow onion

1 small clove garlic, minced

2 tablespoons thinly sliced celery

½ cup chopped fresh tomato

1 tablespoon butter

2 tablespoons diced canned green chilies

3 large eggs

2 tablespoons water

¼ teaspoon salt

⅛ teaspoon ground black pepper

Tabasco or other hot sauce or salsa to taste

1 In a large skillet, combine the onion, garlic, celery, tomato, and ½ tablespoon of the butter. Cook over medium heat until the vegetables soften and the juices nearly evaporate, 7 to 8 minutes. Add the chilies and cook for 1 minute more.

2 In a small bowl, beat the eggs and add the water, salt, and black pepper.

3 Remove the vegetables from the skillet and set them aside. Add the remaining ½ tablespoon of butter to the pan.

4 When the butter has melted, add the egg mixture and cook over low heat until the eggs are softly set, about 3 minutes.

5 Scatter the cooked vegetables on top of the eggs. Tilt the pan away from you, and with a spatula, fold half of the omelet over to enclose the filling. Cook for 30 seconds to heat through.

6 Slide the omelet onto a plate, and if you like, add a few dashes of hot sauce or a dollop of your favorite salsa.

Makes 1 omelet

"**This Florida State alum** and ringside announcer has lost more than seventy-five pounds on a strict low-carb diet, and now he doesn't look so much like ESPN's Bob Ley. Folks on low-carb diets are always looking for something new, and this recipe ain't bad— high praise from an Okie definitely not raised on quiche."

2 teaspoons olive oil

1 cup light cream (or low-fat milk)

1 cup grated cheese (American, cheddar, Parmesan, or Swiss, regular or low-fat varieties)

2 teaspoons dried sweet basil

¼ tablespoon dried paprika

4 eggs (no low-fat substitutes)

Salt to taste

Freshly ground black pepper to taste

1 Oil the bottom and sides of a 9-inch pie plate.

2 Preheat the oven to 325 degrees.

3 In a medium saucepan, heat the cream until scalded, but don't let it boil. Reduce the heat and stir in the grated cheese. When the cheese has melted, stir in the basil and paprika.

4 Remove the saucepan from the heat and cool for 5 minutes. Now add in one egg at a time, mixing thoroughly until all the eggs are used. Add salt and black pepper and mix well.

5 Pour the mixture into the pie plate. Bake until the quiche is set, 45 to 50 minutes. Serve hot or cold.

Makes 5 to 6 servings

JIM CORNETTE'S KENTUCKY CORNED BEEF SANDWICHES

"Master James E. Cornette's eating habits are legendary. In fact, I think the Wendy's triple burger might have been Corney's idea. This guy knows his beef! As a matter of fact, I think James E. and I really bonded after I introduced him to the Whataburger chain and he turned me on to Steak 'n Shake. Jim Cornette is now tutoring future Federation Superstars at Ohio Valley Wrestling in Louisville, Kentucky. This is a great sandwich! Don't use oil-based coleslaw, and try potato bread instead of rye for a change of pace."

1 (3- to 4-pound) uncooked Nathan's or other brand corned beef

Light Done Right Thousand Island dressing

12 slices seedless rye bread

½ pound coleslaw

8 ounces sliced Swiss cheese (reduced fat if desired)

1 Cook the corned beef with the packaged seasoning in a slow cooker, as directed on the package.

2 Remove the corned beef and slice it lengthwise.

3 Spread the Thousand Island dressing on 6 slices of the bread, add the slices of corned beef, and top with the coleslaw and Swiss cheese. Top with the remaining slices of bread and serve immediately.

Makes 6 sandwiches

J.R.'s TEX-MEX STEW

"**This stew is great** on a cold night, and it's even better the next day (always the mark of a good dish)! I prefer to eliminate the corn and chickpeas, which are not on my top-ten vegetable list. Of course, the quality of the meat makes a big difference. Remember, the leaner, the better. This stew is also good if you're taking a long car trip with your buddies, because the black beans can become a good conversation piece."

1½ pounds lean beef chunks
    for stewing

1 cup J.R.'s barbecue sauce
    or your favorite

1 cup bottled salsa

½ (1-ounce) package reduced-
    sodium taco seasoning mix
    (adjust for taste)

½ (7-ounce) can chickpeas

1 cup frozen corn

1 (15-ounce) can black beans

¾ cup freshly chopped cilantro

1 Mix all the ingredients except the beans and cilantro in a 3-quart slow cooker. Cover and cook on high for about 5 hours until beef is very tender.

2 Stir in the beans and cilantro and cook for 1 hour.

3 Serve with rice or tortillas.

Makes 4 servings

HARDY BOYZ' CHICKEN-FRIED STEAK

"**North Carolina natives** Matt and Jeff Hardy lost their mom when they were boys, so these two highflyers learned to cook and sew as youngsters. This dish is in the meat eaters' Hall of Fame, and, ladies, it is indeed the way to a good old boy's heart. Fellas, if your lady can make a main-event chicken-fried steak, you're in luck. And if she can make cream gravy to drown it in, you might want to consider a long-term relationship!"

STEAK:

 ¾ cup flour
 ¼ teaspoon paprika
 ¼ teaspoon salt
 ¼ teaspoon pepper
 1 teaspoon seasoned salt, or to taste
 1½ pounds (4½-inch-thick) rib-eye steaks
 1 large egg, beaten
 ¼ cup cooking oil

GRAVY:

 3 tablespoons drippings
 1¼ cups milk
 3 tablespoons flour
 1 teaspoon salt
 Dash of pepper, or to taste

1 To make the steak, in a medium bowl, combine the flour, paprika, salt, pepper, and seasoned salt.

2 If necessary, hammer the meat with a meat tenderizer to thin and tenderize it. Dip the steaks first in the egg and then in the flour mixture, coating them thoroughly.

3 In a 12-inch skillet, brown the meat in hot oil, turning once. Cover and cook over low heat for 40 minutes or until tender.

4 For the gravy, remove the meat from the oil and pour off all but 3 tablespoons of the drippings. Add ¾ cup of the milk, the flour, salt and pepper and stir until well combined. Cook over medium-low heat until bubbly and thickened and add the remaining ½ cup of milk. Cook 1 to 2 minutes more.

Makes 4 servings and 1¼ cups of gravy

UNDERTAKER'S TURKEY AND SPINACH TETRAZZINI

"**My sources tell me** the 6-foot 10-inch 325-pounder's favorite lady creates this filling and delicious meal quite often, and it always makes the Undertaker happy. And that's the way you want this awesome Superstar to be . . . happy. This is equally good with chicken or turkey—from my personal experience, as this is one of J.R.'s favorite meals, too. Just add a nice salad and you're ready to dine in style."

8 ounces spaghetti, broken into
    4-inch lengths

Salt to taste

1 dead turkey (cut 3 cups bite-size pieces
    of cooked turkey from the carcass)

2 (9-ounce) packages frozen creamed
    spinach, thawed

1 cup part-skim ricotta cheese

½ cup oil-packed sun-dried tomatoes,
    drained and chopped

2 large garlic cloves, minced

10 tablespoons grated Parmesan cheese

Pepper to taste

1 Preheat the oven to 450 degrees.

2 Cook the pieces of spaghetti in a large pot of boiling, salted water until tender. Drain thoroughly, reserving 1 cup of the cooking liquid.

3 In a large bowl, mix the spaghetti, turkey, creamed spinach, ricotta cheese, tomatoes, garlic, 8 tablespoons of the cheese, and the reserved cooking liquid. Season with pepper.

4 Spread the mixture into two 9-inch pie plates and sprinkle with the remaining 2 tablespoons of cheese. Bake 10 minutes, or until the top is a light golden color.

Makes 4 to 6 servings

TASTY TRISH-KEBABS

"**The young lady from Toronto** brings us a tasty treat that is easier to make than the *Gone With the Wind*–length ingredient list would suggest. Trish Stratus is a former big-time fitness model who knows how to eat healthy, and these kebabs fit the bill. Pay attention while cooking this one and you'll get your hand raised at eatin' time. Like Trish, this one is a keeper."

½ cup tomato catsup

¼ cup water

¼ cup finely chopped onion

1 tablespoon brown sugar

3 tablespoons fresh lemon juice (from 1 lemon)

2 tablespoons cooking oil

2 teaspoons prepared mustard

2 teaspoons Worcestershire sauce

½ teaspoon chili powder

1 pound beef tenderloin steak, cut into
    1-inch pieces

½ pound fresh shrimp, shelled

2 zucchini, cut diagonally into 1-inch pieces

2 fresh ears corn, cut into 1-inch rounds

2 small Vidalia or white onions, peeled
    and cut into wedges

½ green pepper, cut into squares

½ red pepper, cut into squares

6 cherry tomatoes

1 Preheat the grill.

2 In a small saucepan, combine the catsup, water, onion, and brown sugar. Stir in the lemon juice, oil, mustard, Worcestershire sauce, and chili powder. Simmer, uncovered, over low heat for 10 minutes, stirring occasionally.

3 On six skewers, thread the steak, shrimp, zucchini, corn, onions, and green and red peppers. Brush with the sauce. Grill the kebabs over medium-hot coals, turning often and brushing with the sauce. Cook to the desired doneness (about 20 minutes for medium).

4 Garnish the ends of the skewers with tomatoes before serving.

Makes 6 servings

"I'll never forget the night Big Show came to my house for dinner. When the 500-pounder sat down at the table, my wife and I didn't breathe for thirty seconds because we were sure the chair would collapse! The Show started eating, and he was **very** hungry, friends. He slammed an entire chicken, a large ham, and close to a quart of apple butter! Luckily, he saved room for a dozen homemade chocolate chip cookies for dessert. The big man likes his food, and you'll like this lamb recipe."

1 (3-pound) lamb roast

1 clove garlic, crushed

1 teaspoon salt

2 tablespoons coarsely ground
    black pepper (or to taste)

1 teaspoon dried basil

½ teaspoon ground ginger

1 bay leaf

½ teaspoon dried thyme

½ teaspoon dried sage

½ teaspoon dried marjoram

1 tablespoon teriyaki sauce
    (or low-salt substitute)

1 tablespoon olive oil

1 Preheat the oven to 350 degrees.

2 Place the meat on a rack in a roasting pan.

3 In a small bowl, combine the rest of the ingredients and mix thoroughly.

4 Make 4½-inch slits in the meat and rub the mixture into the slits and over the entire surface of the meat.

5 Insert a meat thermometer into the thickest part of the meat, and place the pan in the oven. After 10 minutes, reduce the heat to 300 degrees and roast to the desired doneness, 2 to 2¼ hours for medium.

**Makes 1 serving if you're Big Show;
otherwise, makes 4 to 6 servings**

J.R.'S MASHED POTATO MEAT LOAF

"**There's no doubt in my mind** that if I had a very special dinner with my three biggest heroes—my dad, John Wayne, and Mickey Mantle—this would be the entrée. How can you go wrong with meat and potatoes?! Small red potatoes with their skins left on give this stick-to-your-ribs dish great flavor. If I owned a restaurant, this would definitely be on the menu."

1 (12-ounce) jar home-style brown
    beef gravy
1½ pounds lean ground beef
1 cup soft homemade bread crumbs
½ cup finely chopped onions
1 egg, slightly beaten
½ teaspoon salt
¼ teaspoon coarsely ground pepper
2½ cups hot mashed potatoes
1 tablespoon butter, melted
Paprika to taste

1 Preheat the oven to 350 degrees.

2 Combine ½ cup of the gravy with the beef, bread crumbs, onions, egg, salt, and pepper. Shape the mixture into an 8 × 4-inch loaf. Place in a loaf pan and bake for 1 hour.

3 Carefully drain the fat from the pan and discard.

4 Spread the mashed potatoes over the top and sides of the meat loaf. Drizzle the melted butter over the potatoes and sprinkle them with paprika. Bake for an additional 20 minutes, then let stand for 5 minutes.

5 Heat the remaining gravy and serve it with the meat loaf slices.

Makes 6 servings

TRIPLE H'S SWORDFISH À LA HELMSLEY

"**Triple H is one of the most** intelligent and best-conditioned athletes in the business, and he knows as much about nutrition as anyone. He started concentrating on bodybuilding as a teenager, and he has since shown many of his fellow grapplers the correct way to eat. It's important to use **fresh** swordfish and to avoid overcooking because it can get as tough as shoe leather. Old J.R. can also live without the watercress."

1 teaspoon butter or low-fat spray
1½ pounds swordfish steaks
Salt to taste
Freshly ground black pepper to taste
⅛ teaspoon paprika
¼ cup olive oil
2 tablespoons dried sweet or
    regular basil
2 tablespoons fresh lemon juice
Watercress (optional)

1 Grease a broiler rack or broiling pan with the butter and place it about 2 inches below the broiler element. Preheat the broiler.

2 Wash the steaks and sprinkle them with the salt, pepper, and paprika. Place the steaks on the preheated broiler rack.

3 Coat the top of the steaks with half the olive oil and broil for 3 minutes. Turn the steaks over and coat the other side with the remaining olive oil, then sprinkle with the basil. Broil for an additional 4 to 5 minutes.

4 Sprinkle with the lemon juice and, if desired, garnish with watercress.

Makes 3 to 4 servings

BRADSHAW'S SMOTHERED TEXAS ROUND STEAK

"**Bradshaw is the resident** stock (not livestock) expert in the Federation. This big old Texan can hold his own with any stock market analyst, and this all-American red meat dish is truly so good you'll want to package it, take it to Wall Street, and go public with it. Sources say this former Abilene Christian All-American offensive tackle likes to pour on the onions, which sounds like a profitable investment to me."

1 (2-pound) round steak (about ¼ inch thick)

Freshly ground white pepper to taste (or chili powder for extra attitude)

2 teaspoons olive oil

2 medium white onions, peeled and sliced

1 beef bouillon cube and 1 to 1½ cups water, or 1 (12-ounce) can of beer (like Bradshaw makes it)

1 Trim the meat and cut it into 1 × 3-inch slices. Sprinkle it with the white pepper.

2 Preheat a large, nonstick skillet over high heat. Add the oil. In batches if necessary, brown the meat on all sides, about 3 minutes.

3 Add the onions. Add the bouillon cube and enough of the water to cover the bottom of the pan by ¼ inch (or add the beer). Cover, reduce the heat to medium-low, and simmer until tender, 20 to 40 minutes, depending upon the thickness of the meat.

Makes 6 to 8 servings

PAT PATTERSON'S BIG CABBAGE BALLS

"Patterson grew up in a large, poor family in Montreal where cabbage was cheap and plentiful. Pat's French mother had several cabbage recipes but this one was main-event status. I've had these, made by Pat in his home with his late friend Louis Dondero, and they are off the page. So was the conversation with those two. I miss Louie, and my wife makes these from time to time to honor our friend, and the first Intercontinental Champion."

2 to 3 large heads cabbage

2 pounds lean ground beef

1 pound lean ground pork

1 medium onion, chopped fine

1 cup uncooked rice

Salt to taste

Freshly ground black pepper to taste, or your favorite seasoning

2 cups tomato juice

1 In a big pot, boil one cabbage at a time until the leaves are loose. Do not overboil. Remove each cabbage and let it cool while the other cabbages cook.

2 In a large bowl, mix the ground beef, ground pork, onion, rice, salt, and pepper.

3 When the cabbage is cool enough to touch, cut down around the heart as deep as you can so you see all the leaves come loose. Take a leaf, lay it flat, and cut off the tough bottom part of the leaf.

4 *Here's the secret of stuffing the cabbage!* Place the meat and rice mixture on a cabbage leaf—*do not pack the mixture tightly*—and roll the leaf around the mixture to make a ball.

5 Continue to make balls until you run out of the meat mixture. As you finish each ball, put it in a large pot, stacking the balls on top of one another and end to end.

6 When you finish making all the balls, pour the tomato juice on them until they are completely covered.

7 Cover the pot and cook over medium-high heat until the juice starts to boil. Reduce the heat to low and simmer for 2 to 2½ hours. Keep covered tightly. Do *not* cook over high heat, or the balls on the bottom will burn.

Makes about 24 cabbage balls

BIG BOSS MAN'S PEPPER STEAK

"The TV story line in which the Boss Man grilled Al Snow's Chihuahua Pepper is a prime example of the Boss Man's rather *unique* sense of humor."

*(Note: Do **NOT** prepare this recipe! The Boss Man insisted we include it, but the REAL recipe for Pepper Steak is on the next page.)*

The Boss Man says, "This recipe is best for the 'southern-aware' cook, as its preparation is traditional to most southern dishes. Also, I don't advise those with weak stomachs to prepare this dish."

**1 can bacon drippings
  (see instructions below)**
1 live Chihuahua
1 onion, peeled and chopped
1 green bell pepper, seeded and chopped

Bacon drippings: Whenever you fry bacon, pour the drippings into a can. Put the lid on and store it on top of the stove. The drippings will congeal and liquefy over and over again. Continue adding to the drippings whenever you fry bacon, and use when necessary for any recipe.

Dog preparation: Catch it, hold back feet firmly, step on parts. Skin and gut it (you can use the fur for hats, gloves, coat trim, and so on). Boil until the meat falls from the bones. Tear the meat into chunks.

1 Put the drippings, meat, onion, and green pepper in a 8-inch cast-iron skillet.

2 Cook until done or a grease fire begins.

(In future volumes, look for **Pepper Snacks**, **Snoop Doggy Sandwiches**, and **Paw-kabobs**.)

BIG BOSS MAN'S PEPPER STEAK

"This is more like it! Ray Traylor may be known around the world as the Big Boss Man, but this 300-pound Georgian knows a good pepper steak when he sinks his teeth into it. Known as Big Bubba when he first started his rasslin' career, the 6-foot 6-inch veteran is a pretty good cook who has been known to eat a pound and a half of flank steak all by himself."

2 medium red onions, peeled and sliced

1 large red bell pepper, cut into ¼-inch strips

1 large green bell pepper, cut into ¼-inch strips

1 cup tomato juice

1 teaspoon grated lemon zest

1 teaspoon paprika

1 clove garlic, finely chopped

1 cup beef broth

2 tablespoons chopped fresh basil leaves (or 2 teaspoons dried)

2 tablespoons lemon juice

¼ teaspoon salt

Cooking spray

1 (1½-pound) beef flank steak

1 teaspoon olive oil

¼ teaspoon freshly ground black pepper

1 In a 10-inch skillet, cook the onions, bell peppers, tomato juice, lemon zest, paprika, and garlic over medium heat for 5 minutes.

2 Reduce the heat to medium-low and stir in the broth. Cover and cook about 10 minutes, or until the liquid has almost evaporated. Stir in the basil, lemon juice, and salt. Keep warm.

3 Preheat the broiler and spray the broiler pan rack with cooking spray.

4 Trim the fat from the steak. Brush it with olive oil and sprinkle it with pepper.

5 Place the steak on the rack in the broiler pan and broil with the top about 2 to 3 inches from the heat for about 5 minutes, or until brown, turning occasionally. Broil about 5 minutes longer for medium doneness (160 degrees).

6 Cut the beef into thin slices, slicing across the grain at a slanted angle. Top with the onion mixture and serve.

**Makes
6 servings**

J.R.'S SLOBBERKNOCKER PORK CHOPS

"**Back when I was a Young** Oklahoma Future Farmer of America member in Westville, Oklahoma, we never named the porkers on our farm. They weren't pets, they were future pork chops! When I walk in the door after a long day in the office and smell these bad boys in the oven, all is right with the universe. It's one of the world's **great** aromas!"

6 shoulder-cut pork chops, trimmed of fat

1 cup finely mashed frosted shredded wheat

1 tablespoon olive oil

1 large onion, peeled and chopped

1 (16-ounce) can whole tomatoes, undrained

1 teaspoon dry mustard

1 tablespoon brown sugar

Salt to taste

Freshly ground black pepper to taste

Several dashes of Worcestershire sauce

1 Preheat the oven to 350 degrees.

2 Rinse the pork chops and coat them with the shredded wheat.

3 Heat the oil in the skillet over medium heat. Fry the chops and the onion until golden brown.

4 Place the pork chops and the onion in a large baking pan (about 13 × 9 inches). Cover them with the tomatoes (halve large tomatoes if necessary) and add the mustard, brown sugar, salt, pepper, and Worcestershire sauce to taste.

5 Cover with foil and bake for 1 hour. Remove the cover and bake for an additional 15 minutes.

Makes 6 servings

"This is a great way to do chicken on your grill, and a recipe we use at our house quite often. Because the bird is essentially smoked for two and a half hours, it's very healthful. Just remember that all great grill cooks must have patience because this one takes a while to get perfect. The can inserted into the chicken makes a unique visual but an even better pedestal on which your yardbird will smoke perfectly. And don't forget, the cans do get very hot, so handle with care."

J.R.'S ROASTED CHICKEN

2 (4- to 5-pound) chickens
2 tablespoons Sylvia's Secret Chicken Rub
    seasoning (or seasoning of your choice)
Sea salt to taste
Coarsely ground pepper to taste
½ teaspoon paprika
2 half-full (12-ounce) cans beer
Cooking spray

1 Rinse the chickens and pat them dry with paper towels inside and out.

2 Mix the chicken rub seasoning, salt, pepper, and paprika together and rub generously on the chickens, inside and outside.

3 Place the chickens over the open beer cans so that the beer cans are just inside the cavities of the two chickens, and coat the chickens with cooking spray.

4 Carefully stand the chickens on the beer cans on the grill and roast them slowly over medium-low heat until golden brown, about 2½ hours. Check every 20 minutes to adjust the heat and spray the chickens with cooking spray to keep them moist.

Makes 4 servings

THE BROOKLYN BRAWLER'S ARTICHOKE CHICKEN

In memory of Louie Dondero

"**Kimchi.** Knuckleball Schwartz. Doink. The Brooklyn Brawler. All have been Federation vet Steve Lombardi's aliases over the past fifteen years. He's seen it all and probably should write a book. It would be a riot—and perhaps cause a few divorces. Steve still wrestles on occasion and provides valuable support behind the scenes. Much to the Big Apple's chagrin, the Brawler now lives in Detroit, but this recipe was created by Steve's Italian granny in Brooklyn."

4 chicken breasts, cut into strips
Garlic salt to taste
Flour
4 (4-ounce) jars artichoke hearts
2 teaspoons olive oil
½ cup white wine
1 onion, peeled and chopped

1 Preheat the oven to 300 degrees.

2 Sprinkle the chicken strips with garlic salt on both sides and roll them in flour.

3 Drain the oil from the artichoke hearts and set both aside.

4 Heat the olive oil in a frying pan, and add ⅓ of the artichoke oil you've set aside. When hot, add ¼ cup of the white wine.

5 Lay in half of the chicken pieces. Cook over low heat on all sides until the flour cooks into the chicken, but don't brown the chicken. Pour the contents of the frying pan into a roasting pan.

6 Repeat steps 4 and 5 with the next batch of chicken.

7 Add the artichoke hearts and the onion to the roasting pan and cook for 30 minutes, stirring every 10 minutes. Serve over rice.

Makes 4 servings

HARDCORE HOLLY'S
BIG BEEFY MEATBALLS

"**Hardcore Holly eats** *every two to three hours*! That means he *sets his alarm* and wakes up to eat. Hardcore is very serious about his food, and he prepares this recipe when he's looking for plenty of protein. He says the cayenne pepper is good for your heart, too. Hardcore is as physically tough a competitor as any in the Federation, and these meatballs are primo!"

2 pounds ground sirloin

1 onion, diced

1 cup soft bread crumbs

2 eggs

1 cup tomato sauce

¼ cup soy sauce

½ to 1 teaspoon cayenne pepper to taste

Garlic salt to taste

Salt to taste

Freshly ground black pepper to taste

1 Preheat the oven to 375 degrees.

2 Mix all the ingredients together in a bowl and roll the mixture into 1-inch balls.

3 Brown the meatballs in a skillet for 10 minutes then transfer them to a 13 × 9-inch pan and cook, covered, for 40 to 45 minutes.

4 Serve over noodles or rice, eat with some French bread, or serve as an appetizer.

Makes about 24 meatballs

DUDLEY BOYZ' DUDLEYVILLE CHICKEN AND DUMPLINGZ

"Now this is livin'! This is a world-class meal so good I once ate it three days in a row! The dark meat chicken stays moist and tasty, and the more dumplings the better. After trying this dish, you might even feel good enough to attempt a Dudley-like table dive. At the very least you'll get a euphoric look on your face à la Bubba Ray!"

6 chicken thighs, skins removed

1 (8-ounce) package fresh baby carrots

12 white pearl onions, peeled

1 teaspoon dried thyme

¼ teaspoon pepper

Salt to taste

3 (14-ounce) cans chicken broth

1 cup Bisquick

⅓ cup milk

1 Rinse the chicken thighs and place them in a Dutch oven. Cook over medium heat, stirring frequently, for 10 minutes, or until browned.

2 Add the carrots, onions, ½ teaspoon of the thyme, the pepper, and salt, and cook for another 10 minutes on medium-low heat.

3 Add the broth and bring to a boil. Turn the heat to low, cover, and simmer for 30 to 40 minutes.

4 To make the dumplings, mix the Bisquick and the remaining ½ teaspoon thyme in a small bowl, then stir in the milk.

5 Drop tablespoonfuls of the dumpling dough into the stew. Cover and cook over medium heat for 10 minutes. Remove the cover and cook for another 10 minutes.

Makes 4 servings

J.R.'S DEEP-DISH ITALIAN SAUSAGE LASAGNA

"I'm a very lucky man. In addition to being ten years younger than I am and a former gymnast, my beautiful Italian wife is also a wonderful cook! And so was her grandmother, who perfected this recipe decades ago. It's a tried-and-true dish that has been making people smile for years. It's the only lasagna recipe you'll ever need."

2 pounds sweet Italian sausage, crumbled

2 (28-ounce) jars chunky spaghetti sauce

2 (15-ounce) containers ricotta cheese (reduced-fat if desired)

½ cup grated Parmesan cheese

½ cup grated Romano cheese

2 tablespoons chopped fresh Italian flat-leaf parsley

2 tablespoons chopped fresh oregano leaves (or 1 tablespoon dried)

2 (8-ounce) packages (about 20) lasagna noodles, cooked

4 cups shredded, reduced-fat mozzarella cheese

1 Preheat the oven to 375 degrees.

2 In a 12-inch skillet, cook the sausage over medium heat until no longer pink. Drain the fat. Stir in the spaghetti sauce.

3 In a medium bowl, mix the ricotta, Parmesan and Romano cheeses, and the parsley and oregano.

4 Spread 1½ cups of the meat sauce in an ungreased lasagna pan (13 × 9-inch or larger) and cover completely with noodles (about 5).

5 Spread 1⅓ cups of the cheese mixture over the noodles, then add another 1½ cups of the meat sauce on top. Sprinkle with 1 cup of the mozzarella cheese.

6 Repeat the layers twice with 5 noodles, 1⅓ cups of cheese sauce, 1½ cups meat sauce, and 1 cup of mozzarella cheese.

7 Top with the last 5 noodles, and then the remaining sauces. Sprinkle with the remaining mozzarella, Parmesan, and Romano cheeses.

8 Cover and bake 1¼ hours.

9 Uncover and bake 15 minutes more, or until the lasagna is hot throughout and the cheese is golden brown.

10 Let stand, loosely covered, for 15 minutes before serving.

Makes 8 servings

GRILLED STEAK BENOIT

"**Chris Benoit is one of the healthiest** eaters in the World Wrestling Federation, and his regular diet includes an ample amount of steak. If you're ever at the Benoit home for a cookout, don't be surprised if this is your main course, prepared by the Wolverine himself. Growing up in Edmonton, Canada, Chris was a huge wrestling fan who idolized England's Dynamite Kid, Tommy Billington. But as great as Dynamite was before a back injury put him out of business, Benoit is going to be even better. I ain't so sure about the three-day marathon marinade he recommends in this recipe, but I do strongly suggest at least twenty-four hours."

½ cup soy sauce

⅔ cup red wine

½ cup peach preserves

5 cloves garlic

½ medium sweet onion

Pinch of salt

Pinch of freshly ground black pepper

4 steaks (use your favorite kind)

1 Place all the ingredients except the steak into a blender and mix well.

2 Poke the steak with a knife repeatedly to tenderize it.

3 Score the meat on both sides by making shallow cuts in a crisscross pattern.

4 Pour the marinade over the meat, cover it, and leave it in the refrigerator for at least 1 day (3 days is ideal).

5 Remove the meat from the marinade and grill to your liking.

Makes enough sauce for 4 steaks

DEAN MALENKO'S BEEF STROGANOFF

"**Does Dean Malenko remind anyone** else of their high school biology teacher? His dad was 'Professor' Boris Malenko, a brilliant wrestler who portrayed a Russian madman in the squared circle for many years. This recipe is a longtime Malenko family favorite."

1 pound beef tenderloin

4 tablespoons flour

¾ teaspoon salt

4 tablespoons butter or margarine

1½ cups sliced fresh mushrooms

½ cup chopped onion

1 clove garlic, minced

1 tablespoon tomato paste

1 tablespoon instant beef bouillon
   granules

1 cup low-fat sour cream

2 tablespoons dry white wine

8 ounces extra-wide noodles,
   cooked and hot

1 Slice the meat across the grain into thin, bite-size strips.

2 Combine 1 tablespoon of the flour and ½ teaspoon of the salt and coat the meat with the mixture.

3 In a skillet, heat 2 tablespoons of the butter. Add the meat, browning quickly on both sides. Then add the mushrooms, onion, and garlic, and cook 3 to 4 minutes, or until the onion is crisp and tender. Remove from the pan and set aside.

4 Add the remaining 2 tablespoons of butter to the pan drippings and stir in 2 tablespoons of the flour. Add the tomato paste, bouillon granules, and the remaining ¼ teaspoon salt. Stir in 1¼ cups of water and cook over medium-high heat, stirring, until bubbly. Cook and stir 1 to 2 minutes longer.

5 In a small bowl, mix the sour cream and remaining 1 tablespoon of flour.

6 Return the meat and mushroom mixture to the skillet.

7 Stir in the sour cream mixture and the wine. Heat thoroughly, but do not boil.

8 Serve over the noodles.

Makes 4 servings

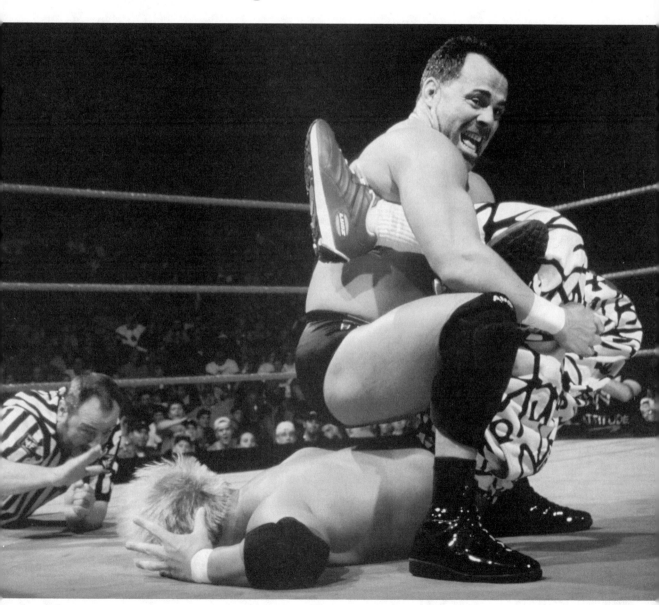

RIKISHI'S RUMP ROAST

"**Rikishi is the first person** in the business whose behind became the star of the show, so his favorite dish had to be a rump roast, didn't it? It's a different approach, but it works. This is a terrific roast that makes a wonderful Sunday family meal, especially when you add a few more spuds."

1 (3- to 4-pound) beef chuck pot roast

Flour for dredging

Vegetable oil

2 medium potatoes or sweet potatoes
    (or 1 of each), peeled and quartered

4 carrots, cut into 1½-inch pieces

Salt to taste

Freshly ground black pepper to taste

¾ cup water, beef broth, dry red wine,
    beer, or tomato juice

½ teaspoon crushed dried basil
    or thyme (more, if desired)

½ teaspoon Worcestershire sauce
    (more, if desired)

1 Trim the excess fat from the meat and coat all sides of the meat with flour. In a heavy sauté pan, brown the meat on all sides for 10 minutes. Add oil if necessary.

2 Place the potatoes and carrots on the bottom of a Crock-Pot and place the meat on top. Cut the meat if necessary to fit.

3 Generously salt and pepper the meat and vegetables.

4 Add the water, basil, and Worcestershire sauce.

5 Cover and cook on low heat for 8 to 10 hours.

Makes 8 servings

KAIENTAI'S STIR-FRY

"**Who else but our two young** Japanese competitors would submit their favorite quick and delicious stir-fry recipe? Growing up on a farm in eastern Oklahoma, I didn't eat a lot of Asian food, but traveling around the world with the World Wrestling Federation has given me the opportunity to sample cuisine from all over the globe. I like it! It's healthy *and* filling. Not a bad tag team."

2 whole skinless chicken breasts (about 12 ounces each)

⅓ cup soy sauce

⅓ cup chicken broth

4 tablespoons peanut or vegetable oil

1 clove garlic, halved

1 small acorn squash, halved, seeded, cubed, and cooked for 5 minutes

1 cup green beans, snipped

1 small yellow squash, sliced

1 cup sliced mushrooms

1 (6-ounce) package frozen Chinese pea pods, thawed

1 (10-ounce) package fresh spinach, washed and trimmed

3 cups shredded Chinese cabbage

1 Cut the chicken into 1-inch pieces. In a glass bowl, mix the pieces with soy sauce and chicken broth and set aside.

2 Set an electric wok to 375 degrees and add 2 tablespoons of the oil. Heat until sizzling. Add the garlic and cook for 2 minutes, then remove and discard it.

3 Remove the chicken from the marinade and drain it on paper towels, reserving the marinade. Cook the chicken quickly in the hot oil, stirring constantly. When cooked through, remove the chicken and keep warm.

4 Add the remaining 2 tablespoons of oil to the wok, then the acorn squash and green beans. Toss until the vegetables glisten with oil, then push them to the side.

5 Add the yellow squash and mushrooms and toss them in oil. Push them to the side.

6 Repeat with the pea pods, spinach, and Chinese cabbage.

7 Return the chicken to the wok with the reserved marinade and toss everything, blending well.

8 Lower the temperature to 200 degrees and cover the wok. Simmer for 5 minutes, or until vegetables are crisp but tender.

9 Serve with steamed rice, if you wish.

Makes 4 servings

DROZ'S BARBECUE CHICKEN PIZZA

"**Since being paralyzed** in an in-ring accident, Droz has displayed the courage of a true champion. He's worked tirelessly in physical therapy, and I fully expect to see him walk again. I really do. A former Maryland Terrapin and Denver Broncos defensive lineman, Droz has the heart of a lion and a drive many of us can only dream about."

1 (10-ounce) package refrigerated
    Pillsbury pizza dough
½ cup J.R.'s BBQ sauce (or your favorite)
2 chicken breasts (about ½ pound),
    grilled and diced
½ medium red bell pepper, sliced
½ medium green bell pepper, sliced
½ medium yellow bell pepper, sliced
1 cup grated mozzarella cheese
1 cup (4 ounces) grated mild
    cheddar cheese

1 Prepare and bake the pizza dough according to the directions on the package.

2 Take the dough out of the oven and spread the barbecue sauce on it. Decorate the pizza with the chicken and peppers and top it with the cheeses.

3 Bake for 10 minutes longer or until the cheeses have melted and are golden in color.

Makes 2 servings

D'LO BROWN'S BASIC BROILED CHICKEN

"**Most people don't know** that D'Lo—who has a CPA degree from the University of Maine—once weighed more than 400 pounds. Now a well-conditioned 265-pounder, D'Lo knows how to eat healthy without feeling hungry afterward. This very simple dish does the trick, and when company is coming over for dinner, it's tough to beat. Of course, I like to dip my chicken in a little J.R.'s BBQ sauce to add sizzle!"

2 broiler-fryer chickens (about 2 pounds each), halved or quartered

½ teaspoon paprika

1 teaspoon poultry seasoning

Salt to taste

Freshly ground black pepper to taste

4 tablespoons (½ stick) butter or margarine, melted (or ¼ cup olive or vegetable oil)

1 Preheat the broiler.

2 Wash the chickens and pat them dry. Sprinkle them with the paprika, seasoning, salt, and pepper and brush them with melted butter.

3 Place the chickens, skin-side down, on a rack in the broiler pan and broil 6 inches from the heat for 20 to 25 minutes, brushing occasionally with the butter.

4 Turn the chickens, brush them with butter, and broil 15 to 20 minutes longer, or until nicely browned.

Makes 4 servings

JERRY LAWLER'S CHICKEN À LA KING

"**A true artist** in every sense of the word, whether on the canvas in the ring or on a painter's canvas à la Norman Rockwell (the King's favorite), Jerry Lawler is one of a kind. I call him the world's oldest teenager (sorry, Dick Clark) because the King is so much fun to be around. He's always 'on,' and so is this Chicken à la King. It may not be as famous in Memphis as Jerry Lawler, but it should be."

4 tablespoons (½ stick) butter or margarine

4 tablespoons flour

2 tablespoons finely chopped onion

1 teaspoon salt

½ teaspoon Worcestershire sauce

2 cups milk

2 cups diced cooked chicken

¼ cup diced pimiento (about 2 pimientos)

1 (3- to 4-ounce) can sliced mushrooms

1 Melt the butter in a medium saucepan. Remove from the heat.

2 Blend in the flour, onion, salt, and Worcestershire sauce. Stir in the milk and cook over low heat, stirring constantly, until the sauce thickens and boils, about 1 minute.

3 Stir in the chicken, pimiento, and mushrooms and heat thoroughly.

4 Serve over hot buttered rice, noodles, or toast, if desired.

Makes 4 servings

MEAN STREET POSSE POT PIE

"Ever notice that **Federation Superstars** eat a lot of chicken? And I mean a *lot* of chicken! This is another idiot-proof recipe (no offense, Posse) that anyone who can turn on an oven can do. But don't start watching *Raw* or *Smackdown!* and forget your pies in the oven. You want these to be golden brown."

> 1⅔ cups frozen mixed vegetables, thawed
>
> 1 cup chopped cooked chicken
>
> 1 (10½-ounce) can condensed cream of chicken soup
>
> 1 egg
>
> ½ cup milk
>
> 1 cup Bisquick

1 Preheat the oven to 400 degrees.

2 Mix the vegetables, chicken, and soup in an ungreased 9-inch pie plate.

3 Stir together the remaining ingredients with a fork until blended. Pour over the chicken mixture.

4 Bake 30 minutes or until golden brown.

Makes 6 servings

The Posse likes to make several potpies and **freeze** what they don't eat. Then they throw the frozen pies through car windows from highway overpasses, but please don't try that at home. This is the Posse's home cookin'. While on tour, however, they like to shovel three scoops of protein powder into their mouths and wash it down with water.

J.R.'S SPICY PORK STEW

"**Ah, pork . . .** the other white meat. One of the first things you learn growing up on a farm is to not get emotionally attached to the livestock because it will probably end up on the supper table. This dish will fill you up *and* clear your sinuses. Add some corn bread and you're there."

1 tablespoon vegetable oil

2¼ pounds pork shoulder or boneless country-style spare ribs, cut into 1-inch cubes

Salt to taste

Freshly ground black pepper to taste

1 large onion, chopped

6 large garlic cloves, chopped

1½ tablespoons chopped jalapeño

2 (14½-ounce) cans Mexican-style stewed tomatoes

1 tablespoon ground cumin

1 tablespoon dried oregano

2 (15-ounce) cans kidney beans, rinsed and drained

1 In a large Dutch oven, heat the oil over high heat.

2 Season the pork with salt and pepper, then add it to the Dutch oven and sauté it until it is no longer pink, about 10 minutes.

3 Add the onion, garlic, and jalapeño and cook 5 minutes. Add the tomatoes with their liquid, cumin, and oregano. Cover and reduce the heat to medium-low and simmer until the pork is tender, about 1 hour.

4 Mix the beans into the stew and simmer until heated thoroughly, about 10 minutes.

5 Season with salt and pepper.

Makes 6 servings

"**The greatest box-office attraction in** the history of our business makes a helluva rib rub. As with any marinade, the longer you leave it on your choice of meat, the better. Some folks really like dry rub, and this one is easy to master, unlike Stone Cold himself. (Note: No rattlesnakes are harmed in its creation.)

"Use on pork chops, ribs, or steaks."

2 tablespoons coarsely ground
     black pepper

1 teaspoon salt

2 tablespoons sweet paprika

1 teaspoon chili powder

1 tablespoon sugar

1 teaspoon onion powder

1½ teaspoons garlic powder

½ teaspoon dry mustard

1 In a small bowl, stir together all the ingredients. Use immediately or store in a container for up to 1 month.

2 Rub into the meat. Let the meat stand 30 minutes at room temperature or refrigerate 2 to 8 hours before grilling.

**Makes
enough for
4 pork chops
or steaks, or
1 rack of ribs**

STONE COLD'S "STOMP A MUD HOLE IN YOUR STEAKS AND RIBS" SIMMERING SAUCE

"Oh, hell, yeah! Now you're talking friends and neighbors! This could be the meaning of life itself. I equate Stone Cold's sauce with the most profound works of any of the world's great philosophers, and I suspect the Good Lord probably serves this in heaven.

"Use on pork shoulder, steaks, or pork chops."

2 cups bottled chili sauce

¼ cup cider vinegar

1½ cups beer

1 medium onion, finely chopped

½ cup molasses

2 garlic cloves, minced

¼ cup hickory-flavored barbecue sauce (or J.R.'s BBQ sauce)

¼ cup Worcestershire sauce

1 teaspoon hot pepper sauce, or to taste

1 In a medium saucepan, bring all the ingredients except the hot pepper sauce to a boil. Reduce the heat to medium-low and simmer, uncovered, until slightly thickened, about 15 minutes.

2 Stir in the hot pepper sauce.

3 Brush the sauce on the meat in the last 15 minutes of grilling.

4 The sauce can be refrigerated for up to two weeks.

Makes 4 cups, enough for 3 pounds of meat

SHANE MCMAHON'S BROILED SMACKDOWN SCAMPI

"**Okay, Mr. McMahon's only son** is just a little bit hyper. He's never tried Sanka. So this tasty shrimp dish really works for Shane because it doesn't take long to complete. Even Shane-O-Mac can handle four minutes of cooking time! Don't be afraid to add more garlic. It's good for you."

6 tablespoons (¾ stick) unsalted butter, at room temperature

¼ cup olive oil

1 tablespoon minced garlic

1 tablespoon minced onion

1 tablespoon minced shallots

2 tablespoons snipped fresh chives

¼ teaspoon paprika

Salt to taste

Freshly ground black pepper to taste

2 pounds large shrimp, peeled and deveined

1 Preheat the broiler.

2 In a large bowl, combine all the ingredients except the shrimp. Blend thoroughly.

3 Toss the shrimp in the mixture until thoroughly coated.

4 Broil the shrimp as close to the flame as possible for 2 minutes on each side, or until pink.

5 Serve immediately.

Variation: Here's the Smackdown part of the recipe. Sprinkle some extra garlic either into the marinade sauce or directly on the shrimp.

Makes 4 servings

CHRISTIAN'S EGGPLANT PARMIGIANA

"This is an excellent dish that doesn't need anything to make it better . . . much like Christian. Incidentally, the word *eggplant* is widely used in wrestle-speak to mean a wrestler who is not very bright."

¼ cup flour

½ teaspoon salt

1 medium eggplant, peeled and cut crosswise into ¼-inch slices

1 egg, beaten

¼ cup cooking oil

⅓ cup grated Parmesan cheese

1 (16-ounce) jar spaghetti sauce

6 ounces mozzarella cheese slices, cut into triangles

1 Preheat the oven to 400 degrees.

2 Combine the flour and salt.

3 Dip the eggplant first into the egg, then into the flour mixture.

4 Brown the eggplant in hot oil for 3 minutes per side, adding oil as needed. Drain well on paper towels.

Makes 6 servings

5 Place half the eggplant slices in a single layer in a medium baking dish, cutting the slices to fit, if necessary. Sprinkle with half of the Parmesan cheese. Top with half of the spaghetti sauce and half of the mozzarella.

6 Repeat step 5 with the remaining ingredients.

7 Bake uncovered for 10 to 15 minutes, or until hot.

JACQUELINE'S LUSCIOUS STUFFED GREEN PEPPERS

"**Talk about stuffed green peppers**—Miss Jackie knows her groceries! This Texas lady is very independent and tougher than an IRS audit. Even if you don't like green peppers, don't tap out. Throw the pepper away and devour the filling."

6 large green bell peppers

1 teaspoon salt, plus additional
    for sprinkling peppers

1 pound lean ground beef

½ cup chopped onion

1 (16-ounce) can tomatoes, chopped,
    with liquid

½ cup long-grain rice

½ cup water

1 teaspoon Worcestershire sauce

Freshly ground black pepper to taste

1 cup (4 ounces) shredded low-fat
    American cheese

1 Preheat the oven to 350 degrees.

2 Cut the top ½ inch from the green peppers. Discard the seeds and membranes and chop the top to make ¼ cup. Set aside.

3 Boil the whole green peppers, uncovered, for 5 minutes. Invert them and drain well.

4 Lightly sprinkle the insides of the peppers with salt. In a skillet, cook the beef, onion, and chopped pepper tops over medium-low heat until the meat is browned and the vegetables are tender. Drain off excess fat.

5 Add the tomatoes, uncooked rice, water, 1 teaspoon salt, the Worcestershire sauce, and a dash of black pepper. Bring to a boil, then reduce the heat.

6 Cover and simmer 15 to 18 minutes, or until the rice is tender. Stir in the cheese.

7 Stuff the peppers with the meat mixture, place them in a baking dish, and bake for 30 to 35 minutes or until browned on top.

Makes 6 servings

EDDIE GUERRERO'S MEXICAN TORTILLA CASSEROLE

"**Serving up food for a large family** in El Paso, Eddie Guerrero's mama was a main-event cook, and she still is at age seventy-plus! I'm not saying this casserole is Mama Guerrero quality, but it's very good—and it's a recipe any guy can master. A great dish to enjoy while watching XFL Football."

2 (14½-ounce) cans Mexican-style stewed tomatoes

⅔ cup chopped fresh cilantro

5 (6-inch) corn tortillas

1½ cups (6 ounces) grated Monterey Jack cheese (reduced-fat, if desired)

1½ cups (6 ounces) grated Monterey Jack cheese with jalapeños

Low-fat sour cream to taste

¼ cup sliced pitted black olives (optional)

1 Preheat the oven to 450 degrees.

2 Purée the tomatoes with their juices and ⅓ cup of the cilantro in the food processor.

3 Spread ½ cup of the tomato sauce in the bottom of an 8-inch glass pie plate. Top with one tortilla. Combine the two cheeses and sprinkle ⅔ cup of the mixture over the tortillas. Spoon ½ cup sauce over the cheese.

4 Repeat this layering 3 more times, using 1 tortilla, ⅔ cup cheese, and ½ cup sauce for each layer. Top with the remaining tortilla, sauce, and cheese.

5 Bake until the cheese melts and the sauce bubbles, about 10 minutes.

6 Sprinkle with the remaining ⅓ cup cilantro and garnish with sour cream and olives, if desired.

7 Cut into wedges and serve immediately. Olé!

Makes 4 servings

J.R. AND JAN ROSS'S AWESOME OSSO BUCO

"I don't suppose I'll ever be on death row and have to request a last meal, but if I were, this just might be it! You probably thought old J.R. would order up chicken-fried steak or some ribs, but folks, let me tell you, this is completely off the page. Wrestlemania level. Daddy like!"

¾ cup flour

Salt to taste

Freshly ground black pepper to taste

8 (2-inch-thick) veal shanks
      (6 to 8 pounds total)

¼ cup olive oil

4 tablespoons (½ stick) unsalted butter

2 onions, peeled and coarsely chopped

6 large cloves garlic, peeled and
      chopped

½ teaspoon dried basil

½ teaspoon dried oregano

1 (28-ounce) can Italian plum
      tomatoes, drained

2 cups dry white wine

2 cups beef broth

Zest of 1 lemon

¾ cup chopped fresh Italian flat-leaf
      parsley

1 Preheat the oven to 350 degrees.

2 Season the flour with salt and pepper and dredge the pieces of veal shank in it. Shake off any excess.

3 Heat the oil and butter in a large, flameproof casserole or Dutch oven and sear the veal over medium-high heat. Brown well on both sides. Transfer the veal to paper towels to drain.

4 Add the onions, garlic, basil, and oregano to the casserole and cook over medium heat, stirring occasionally, for 10 minutes, or until the onions are translucent.

5 Add the tomatoes, salt, and pepper. Cook over medium-low heat for another 10 minutes.

6 Add the wine, then raise the heat and bring to a boil. Reduce the heat and simmer, uncovered, for 15 minutes.

7 Return the veal shanks to the casserole and add the beef broth to cover the meat. Transfer the casserole to the oven, and bake, covered, for 1½ hours. Then remove the lid and bake until the veal is very tender, about another 30 minutes.

8 Add half the lemon zest and half the parsley and cook for another 10 minutes.

9 Just before serving, sprinkle with the remaining parsley and lemon zest.

Makes 4 to 5 servings

THE BIG VALBOWSKI'S KIELBASA

"**The best part about this recipe** is that you still have four beers left from the six-pack! (Only kidding.) The best kielbasa I ever had was in Milwaukee. Unfortunately I ate three (okay, four) and had a bit of the old bellyache. Mama always said, 'In moderation, son. In moderation.' This really isn't a great date meal unless your date is from Wisconsin."

4 tablespoons (½ stick) butter
5 small onions, peeled and thinly sliced
1 (2-pound) kielbasa (a big one)
2 (12-ounce) cans beer

1 In a large, heavy skillet, melt the butter and sauté the onions over medium heat until translucent.

2 Add the kielbasa and brown for 4 minutes on each side.

3 Pour the beer over the sausage and onions. Bring to a boil, reduce the heat, and simmer, uncovered, for 25 minutes.

4 Remove the kielbasa and onions from the pan and put them on a serving dish in a warm oven.

5 Over high heat, simmer the beer to reduce it to 2 cups. Pour over the kielbasa and serve.

Makes 4 to 6 servings

THE KAT'S HOMEMADE BEEF JERKY

"**She's a country girl** who's been making homemade jerky since she was a pup, but she's known to millions of fans as Miss Kitty and, simply, the Kat. To those of us who know her well, she's the 'significant other' of Jerry 'the King' Lawler. A true Southern belle, Stacy Carter is a hairstylist by trade and can often be found on the beautiful beaches of Sanibel searching for shells."

1 pound lean beef (such as flank, steak, or brisket)

2 tablespoons Worcestershire sauce

½ cup Original Allegro marinade

2 tablespoons A.1. steak sauce

1 tablespoon soy sauce

½ teaspoon garlic salt

½ teaspoon onion salt

Salt to taste

Freshly ground black pepper to taste

1 Trim the fat from the beef and cut the meat with the grain into long, thin pieces.

2 Combine the Worcestershire sauce, Allegro, A.1., and soy sauce in a gallon-size Ziploc bag.

3 Sprinkle garlic salt, onion salt, salt, and pepper on both sides of the steak.

4 Place the beef strips into the bag and shake to coat them well. Place the bag in the refrigerator for 2 hours.

5 Take the strips from the bag and put them into a dehydrator for 11 to 12 hours.

Makes 1 pound

Note: The longer the beef is dehydrated, the crispier the jerky will be. For a juicier and more tender beef jerky, dehydrate for only 10 hours.

STEVE BLACKMAN'S SERIOUS MARINARA SAUCE

"**This is serious healthy sauce,** and it's even better if you toss in some more garlic. Steve, who eats six to eight times a day, eats plenty of pasta every day before 3 P.M., and this sauce gives any pasta personality. As with an open box of baking soda, it's good to always have some of this sauce in the fridge. Makes chicken breasts better, too. Serious Mr. Blackman has even been rumored to grin a little while enjoying this sauce."

3 tablespoons olive oil

2 onions, peeled and chopped

1 clove garlic, peeled and minced

2½ cups peeled, seeded, and diced tomatoes

¼ teaspoon crumbled dried oregano

¼ teaspoon sugar

Pinch of crumbled dried basil

Salt to taste

Freshly ground black pepper to taste

1 Heat the oil in a heavy medium-size saucepan over medium heat.

2 Add the onions and garlic and sauté until translucent, about 5 minutes. Add the tomatoes, oregano, sugar, and basil and simmer until thickened, stirring occasionally, about 1 hour.

3 Season with salt and pepper.

Makes about 6 cups of sauce

STEVE REGAL'S FISH AND CHIPS

"**Having left home** at age fifteen to join a carnival, where he took on all comers in no-holds-barred fighting, Steve Regal has seen and done it all. The Blackpool, England, native certainly knows his fish and chips, so let the frying begin!"

½ **cup flour**

½ **cup flat English ale**

1 **tablespoon malt vinegar, plus extra for serving**

½ **teaspoon baking soda**

Salt to taste

Freshly ground black pepper to taste

Vegetable oil for frying

1 **(12-ounce) ½-inch-thick cod fillet, cut crosswise into 8 strips**

1 In a medium bowl, whisk the flour, ale, 1 tablespoon malt vinegar, and baking soda until well blended. Season generously with salt and pepper. Cover and let stand at room temperature.

2 Pour the oil into a heavy medium-sized skillet to the depth of ½ inch and heat it to 350 degrees.

3 Pat the fish strips dry with paper towels and season them with salt and pepper.

4 Dip 4 fish strips into the batter, letting the excess drain back into the bowl.

5 Add the fish to the skillet and fry them on both sides until brown and just cooked through, about 3 minutes per side. Transfer them to paper towels.

6 Repeat with the remaining fish.

7 Arrange the fish on a platter and serve with malt vinegar.

Makes 2 servings

"**You really don't need** much more than salt and pepper to make these bad boys righteous. Harvey has been known to whip these up in the old single-wide on the outskirts of Walls, Mississippi. I've been eating these patties—a southern thing—since I was a kid, and Harvey says he makes them every Friday! If old Harve can do it, so can you."

1 (14-ounce) can salmon, undrained

2 eggs

1 cup crushed Premium crackers

Any spices (salt, pepper, seasoned salt, for example)

Vegetable oil for frying

1 Blend the salmon, eggs, crackers, and spices and make the mixture into 3-inch patties.

2 Fry the patties in a small amount of oil until golden brown. Serve with tartar sauce.

Makes 6 patties

HARVEY WHIPPLEMAN'S
SOUTHERN SALMON PATTIES

LEAN AND MEAN: Just as Fun,

Lighter Fare— with Less Fat

JERRY LAWLER'S "FIT FOR A KING" LOW-FAT CHICKEN GUMBO

"**To many folks** in Memphis, Tennessee, Jerry Lawler is a bigger 'King' than Elvis. From headlining sellout events in the Mid-South Coliseum week after week to his infamous confrontations with the late comedian Andy Kaufman—he even played himself in *Man on the Moon*—the King has long been one of sports entertainment's brightest stars and is certainly the favorite broadcast pardner of yours truly. Not bad for a guy who makes a living shouting 'Puppies! Puppies!' on *Raw*. The Kat provided this recipe with conviction, it being one of the King's favorites. He's a very picky eater, so you know this one is very good."

1 pound boneless, skinless chicken breast

2 (15-ounce) cans chicken broth (fat-free, if you prefer)

1 (10-ounce) bag cut frozen okra

2 (15-ounce) cans of Bush's green beans

1 (15-ounce) can corn

1 (15-ounce) can black-eyed peas or purple-hull peas

1 tablespoon dried onions or 1 small onion, chopped

½ teaspoon garlic salt

1 (8-ounce) can chopped tomatoes (optional)

2 cups rice

1 Place the chicken and chicken broth in a large pot. Add water to cover and cook for 30 minutes on medium-high heat. Remove the chicken to cool.

2 Add the vegetables and seasonings to the pot (plus the undrained tomatoes, if desired).

3 Cut the chicken into bite-size pieces and add them to the pot. Cook over medium-high heat for 20 minutes.

4 In a separate pot, cook the rice, following the directions on the package. Stir the rice into the gumbo. (Note: If you want soup instead of gumbo, use less rice.)

Makes 8 servings

VINCE'S BIG BROILED GRAPEFRUITS

"**Mr. 'Mac Man'** has often said to our *Raw* and *Smackdown* television viewers that he 'has the biggest grapefruits' around. I think we should take Vince's word for it on that one, but his recipe for Big Broiled Grapefruits is almost as unique as he is. Just think of this recipe as a tasty conversation piece, especially when you explain its origin to your guests."

3 large grapefruits, at room temperature
3 teaspoons butter or margarine
3 tablespoons brown sugar
¾ teaspoon ground cinnamon
6 maraschino cherries

1 Halve the grapefruits, then cut a thin slice from the bottom of each so that they balance.

2 Cut around each grapefruit half to loosen the fruit from the shell. Remove the cores.

3 Dot each half with ½ teaspoon butter or margarine. Combine the brown sugar and cinnamon and sprinkle them over the grapefruits.

4 Place the grapefruits on the broiler rack or in shallow baking pan, and broil 4 inches from the heat for about 8 minutes, or until they are heated thoroughly and the tops are bubbly.

5 Garnish with maraschino cherries.

Makes 6 servings

IVORY'S ONE-PAN FISH DINNER

"**Most of us know** Ivory can talk a mile a minute, has great energy, and stays very fit. One of the reasons is her diet: lots of fresh fish—the more fish, the more energy. According to Ivory, this recipe is foolproof.

"Ivory says, 'Wanna be lean? Eat fish instead of all that chicken and beef. It's easy!'"

2 medium fillets white fish (such as sea bass, halibut, snapper, or flounder)

¼ cup Caesar salad dressing

Freshly ground black pepper (optional)

1 tablespoon olive oil

2 cups sliced fresh vegetables (bell peppers, carrots, broccoli, spinach, asparagus—gotta get one dark green veggie in there for health!)

1 Lightly coat the fish fillets with the Caesar dressing and pepper.

2 Heat the olive oil in a medium to large skillet.

3 Lay the fish in the skillet and add the vegetables.

4 Cover and cook over medium-low heat until the fish is cooked thoroughly, about 15 minutes. Stir if necessary.

Makes 2 servings

"No one, male or female, has endured more physical challenges training for a career in the ring than Tori. The Wyoming native survived in the Japanese Women's Dojo, widely known as one of the toughest in the world. Tori is also a yoga advocate and one of the 'cleanest eaters' in the Federation. This chicken dish has really got personality and works best on a grill, but it can be broiled, too."

3 tablespoons pure maple syrup

3 tablespoons bottled chili sauce

½ to 1 tablespoon cider vinegar

1 or 2 teaspoons country-style Dijon mustard

4 skinless, boneless chicken thighs

1 tablespoon vegetable oil

Salt to taste

Freshly ground black pepper to taste

1 Preheat the grill to medium-high heat.

2 In a small saucepan, blend the maple syrup, chili sauce, vinegar, and mustard.

3 Brush the chicken with the oil and season it with salt and pepper.

4 Place the chicken on the barbecue and grill it until cooked thoroughly, turning occasionally and brushing generously with the sauce, about 10 minutes.

Makes 4 servings

TORI'S MAPLE BARBECUE CHICKEN

PAUL BEARER'S TUNA-STUFFED TOMATOES

"**After having lost** more than 100 pounds, Paul was quick to contribute this very healthful dish. Kids especially like eating out of the tomato cups. Paul used to like eating out of anything when he weighed about 400 pounds! This George Jones devotee is looking to stay healthy and lose even more pounds, so these stuffed tomatoes are a popular item in the Bearer household."

½ **cup chopped celery**

¼ **cup sliced scallions, green and white parts**

1 **tablespoon fresh lemon juice**

¼ **teaspoon salt**

Freshly ground black pepper to taste

1 **(6½-ounce) can tuna, drained and flaked**

⅓ **cup lite mayonnaise or low-fat salad dressing**

2 **hard-boiled eggs, chopped**

4 **tomatoes**

1 Combine the celery, scallions, lemon juice, and salt, and add a dash of pepper.

2 Stir in the tuna, mayonnaise, and eggs. Cover and chill.

3 When ready to serve, slice the tops off the tomatoes and remove the seeds and core. Without cutting all the way through the tomatoes, cut them into 4 to 6 wedges. Fill each tomato cup with about ½ cup of the tuna mixture.

Makes 4 servings

FAAROOQ'S LOW-FAT "FRIED" CHICKEN

"**Faarooq (Ron Simmons)** grew up eating his grannie's southern fried cooking in Warner Robbins, Georgia. After earning All-American honors on the gridiron at Florida State University and playing some pro football, Ron got into pro wrestling and began to train hard to perfect his physique. Reducing his fat intake was an important part of his new diet, and this recipe is one of his favorites."

Light vegetable oil cooking spray

6 skinless chicken legs

3 chicken breasts, skinned and halved

3½ cups ice water

1 cup plain low-fat yogurt

1 cup Italian bread crumbs

1 cup all-purpose flour

1 tablespoon Old Bay seasoning

½ teaspoon Creole seasoning or Paul Prudhomme's Magic Seasoning Blend

½ teaspoon freshly ground black pepper

Dash of cayenne pepper

½ teaspoon dried thyme

½ teaspoon dried basil

½ teaspoon dried oregano

1 Preheat the oven to 400 degrees.

2 Coat a baking sheet with 5 sprays of the vegetable oil.

3 Put the chicken and ice water in a large bowl. Put the yogurt in a medium bowl. Set both bowls aside.

4 Toss all the remaining ingredients into a large Ziploc bag. Seal and shake well to mix.

5 Remove 2 pieces of chicken from the ice water. Pat them dry and roll them in the yogurt. Put the pieces into the plastic bag, reseal it, and shake it to coat the chicken thoroughly. Transfer the breaded chicken to the baking sheet.

6 Repeat the process until all 12 pieces are breaded.

7 Spray the chicken lightly with the vegetable oil. Place the baking sheet on the bottom shelf of the oven and bake for 1 hour, turning the pieces of chicken every 20 minutes so that they brown evenly.

Makes 4 servings

MICHAEL HAYES'S "P.S." POTATO SKINS

"**When not playing air guitar** or telling 'Fabulous Freebird' stories, our friend Mike (a.k.a. Dok Hendriks) likes to put away the groceries. In addition to broadcasting, Michael works with young wrestlers behind the scenes on their in-ring maneuvers, promos (speaking on the microphone), and strategies. Michael also sweats more than anyone I know, but that's another story. And remember old J.R.'s rule of thumb: If it's a potato, it can't be bad."

6 medium potatoes

3 chicken breasts

4 strips turkey bacon

3 scallions, white and green parts, chopped

1½ cups (6 ounces) shredded mixed (mild and sharp) cheddar cheese

Jalapeño peppers, seeded and chopped, to taste

2 fresh tomatoes, diced

Low-fat sour cream to taste

Fresh tomato salsa to taste

1 Preheat the oven to 350 degrees.

2 Prick the potatoes with a fork, wrap in foil, and bake for 1 hour. Slice them in half lengthwise and scoop out the insides. (Discard the insides or save for another recipe.) Leave the oven on.

3 While the potatoes are baking, grill or sauté the chicken breasts until they are cooked through, and cut them into strips.

4 Cook the turkey bacon according to the directions on the package.

5 Place the potatoes skin-side down on a baking sheet. Divide the cooked chicken and bacon evenly into the potato skins, then add the scallions, cheese, and peppers. Bake for 15 to 20 minutes or until the cheese melts.

6 Top with the tomatoes, sour cream, and salsa.

Makes 4 servings

TAG-TEAM Side Dishes

CLASSICS: and Breads

J.R.'S "SMASHED-DOWN" POTATOES WITH ATTITUDE

"**Old J.R. loves mashed potatoes!** No, I mean I *really love* mashed potatoes. As a matter of fact, I'm sure that somewhere in our world mashed spuds are the basis for a religious sect. Leave the skins on your spuds to enhance the flavor, and use plenty of butter, folks. And forget about using skim milk if you're serious about your mashed potatoes."

3 pounds red potatoes, cubed
Cloves from 1 large head garlic
3 tablespoons half-and-half (or milk)
4 tablespoons unsalted butter
½ teaspoon freshly ground black pepper
Salt to taste

1 Boil the potatoes in a large saucepan for 20 minutes.

2 In a small saucepan, sauté the whole garlic cloves for 15 minutes until soft. Drain the garlic and cool.

3 Drain the potatoes and return them to the saucepan.

4 Slip the skins from the garlic and purée the garlic and the half-and-half in a food processor or blender until smooth.

5 Add the puréed garlic, butter, pepper, and salt to the potatoes. Beat them with a mixer (*not* a food processor or blender) until smooth.

Makes 6 servings

TOO COOL'S "HOMEBOY" FRIES

"**Scotty and Grand Master** came up with a unique way to prepare spuds. I have deep feelings for potatoes and when I first saw these, I thought, What in the heck happened to my spuds? Well, I was surprised that they were very good. I think they're even better with just a little more onion. The Dallas Cowboys may be America's team, but potatoes are the Good Lord's vegetables."

4 baking potatoes, scrubbed and
    patted dry
3 tablespoons olive oil
1 large onion, peeled, halved,
    and thinly sliced
Freshly ground black pepper to taste
Coarse sea salt to taste
½ teaspoon Cajun seasoning

1 Preheat the oven to 350 degrees.

2 Prick the potatoes with a fork, place them on a baking sheet, and bake for 1 hour. Allow them to cool.

3 Leaving the skins on, cut the potatoes into ¼-inch-thick slices.

4 Heat 2 tablespoons of the oil in a large skillet. Add the onion and cook over medium-high heat, turning with a metal spatula, until lightly browned, 8 to 10 minutes.

5 Add the potatoes and cook, turning with a spatula, until they are crisp and brown (adding the extra 1 tablespoon oil if necessary), about 10 minutes.

6 Add the seasonings.

Makes 4 to 6 servings

GRAND MASTER SEXAY'S SWEET POTATO CASSEROLE

"**If Grand Master Sexay** is really the talented young son of wrestling legend Jerry 'the King' Lawler, one has to believe this sweet potato dish was a big hit in their Memphis home. I was never a big fan of sweet potatoes while growing up. One night Mama made them and put a load of melted marshmallows all over the top, hoping to trick me into eating them. Dad had a rule: If you don't clean your plate, there'll be no dessert. I wanted that dessert so I ate the marshmallows and hid the sweet potatoes under some chicken skin, but I still got busted! And, of course, no dessert. Damned sweet potatoes!"

POTATO MIXTURE:

    3 cups cooked sweet potatoes
        (4 to 5 medium potatoes)
    1 cup granulated sugar
    ½ cup (1 stick) butter
    2 eggs
    1 teaspoon vanilla
    ⅔ cup evaporated milk

TOPPING:

    1 cup brown sugar
    ½ cup flour
    ⅓ cup butter
    1 cup chopped pecans

1 Preheat the oven to 325 degrees.

2 To make the potato mixture, beat the cooked potatoes with an electric mixer. Add the granulated
sugar, butter, eggs, vanilla, and milk, and beat until
smooth. Pour the mixture into a shallow pan.

3 To make the topping, combine the ingredients
and sprinkle over the potato mixture.

4 Bake for 30 to 40 minutes,
or until golden.

**Makes 4 to 6
servings**

"I'm not quite sure which Dudley provided this recipe, but I think it was Devon, who eats a little healthier than Brother Bubba. Devon says this dish is so good it will make you stand up and say 'Testify!'"

DUDLEY BOYZ' BAKED SWEET POTATOEZ

4 medium sweet potatoes

Olive oil

Butter to taste

Cinnamon to taste

Brown sugar to taste

1 Preheat the oven to 350 degrees.

2 Wash the sweet potatoes, pat them dry, and place each of them on a square of aluminum foil. Drizzle olive oil over them, coating them lightly. Pierce them with a fork about 4 times, then wrap the foil around them and seal.

3 Bake for 1 hour, or until cooked through. To check doneness, pierce them with the fork.

4 Top them with butter, cinnamon, and brown sugar. Serve immediately.

Makes 4 servings

TONY GAREA'S
VEGETABLES AND WINE OVER RICE

"**Auckland, New Zealand's** contribution to the World Wrestling Federation has enjoyed fine cuisine all over the world and offers this delectable dish for your enjoyment. Tony, a former Federation Tag Team Champion and current road agent, is one of the healthiest eaters around and still trains regularly even though he has been retired from in-ring competition for years. Tony has been known to entertain his lady friends with a romantic home-cooked meal, and this delicious healthful dish is often a part of the presentation. It's good. It's healthful. It's easy to prepare. Go for it!"

1 tablespoon olive oil

1 tablespoon butter

1 large onion, sliced

1 green bell pepper, chopped
   into large pieces

10 medium mushrooms, sliced

1 medium eggplant, cubed

1 (14-ounce) can beef or vegetable broth

½ teaspoon salt

1 tablespoon soy sauce

2 tablespoons cornstarch

2 tablespoons water

½ cup red wine

3 tomatoes, peeled and cut into sixths

3 cups hot cooked rice

1 In a large frying pan, heat the olive oil and butter. Add the onion, pepper, mushrooms, and eggplant and sauté until the onion is translucent, about 10 minutes.

2 Add the broth, salt, and soy sauce. Simmer for 5 minutes.

3 In a small bowl, blend the cornstarch and water. Stir it into the vegetable mixture. Add the red wine and tomatoes. Simmer about 10 minutes more, until the mixture thickens. Season to taste.

4 Serve over the rice. Garlic bread goes well on the side.

Makes 6 servings

"**Mr. Ass is a gifted athlete** with a world-class physique and an intense, competitive nature. Some say too intense. Maybe the Assman is a little tightly wound, but he sure can motor in the old squared circle. Keep an eye on him because even we don't know for sure what he'll do next. Same thing with cooking asparagus on the grill: Keep an eye on them because they must be turned frequently. You don't want them to look like melted plastic straws!"

2 bunches of large or small asparagus, tough bottom stalks snapped off

1 tablespoon olive oil

1 teaspoon seasoned salt

Salt to taste

Freshly ground black pepper to taste

1 Rinse the asparagus, pat dry, and place the spears on a platter. Drizzle it with olive oil, then sprinkle it with seasoned salt, salt, and pepper. Rub the seasonings to coat the asparagus well.

2 Place the asparagus on the upper rack of the grill on medium-low heat, turning occasionally. Cook until slightly blackened, about 10 minutes.

Makes 6 servings

ROAD DOGG'S FRIED GREEN TOMATOES

"**You don't have to be** a hotheaded redneck to enjoy the ultra-talented Road Dogg's fried green tomatoes, but it might help. This is a pure southern delicacy that usually creates a great deal of conversation at suppertime because it's so unique and 'down home.' You owe it to yourself to try this one at least once."

½ cup stone-ground wholewheat flour

½ cup grated Parmesan cheese

¼ teaspoon cayenne pepper

¼ teaspoon freshly ground black pepper

⅛ teaspoon salt

1 cup buttermilk

1 cup canola or olive oil

2 medium green tomatoes, sliced

1 On a plate, blend the flour, cheese, cayenne pepper, black pepper, and salt.

2 Pour the buttermilk into a large, shallow bowl.

3 In a large, heavy skillet, heat the oil over medium-high heat.

4 Dip the tomato slices into the buttermilk and then dredge them in the flour mixture to coat them, shaking off the excess flour.

5 Fry the tomatoes in batches until they are crisp and golden brown, 1 to 2 minutes per side.

Makes 4 servings

BULLDOG'S GREEN BEANS WITH GARLIC

"**Lots of the Federation's** best-conditioned athletes eat a pickup-truckload of garlic, especially the Bulldog. At age fifteen, the British Bulldog Davyboy Smith was wrestling professionally in his hometown of Manchester, England. And at age thirty-six, the UK strongman is still kicking! If you can use fresh green beans, you'll put smiles on faces."

½ cup water
Salt
1 pound fresh green beans, trimmed
4 tablespoons (½ stick) butter or margarine
1 clove garlic, peeled and crushed
Freshly ground black pepper to taste

1 In a deep skillet, add the water, a pinch of salt, and the green beans. Cover and cook over high heat until the beans are barely tender, about 3½ minutes. Place the beans in a serving dish and cover to keep them warm.

2 In a small saucepan over medium heat, melt the butter with the garlic.

3 Pour the mixture over the beans. Add a pinch of salt, and pepper to taste.

Makes 3 to 4 servings

AL SNOW PEAS

"**Unlike Al,** this is a very stable, sane vegetable dish. Yes, Al is vegetablelike, according to Mick Foley, but I'm sure you'll enjoy Al Snow Peas, especially if you like pine nuts. Al's in-ring persona is somewhat nutty, but this seventeen-year veteran is a very talented performer with a warped sense of humor. Mick Foley says Al does some unique tricks with leftover snow peas. Don't ask, kids."

3 tablespoons sesame oil

1 pound snow peas, trimmed

10 thin scallions, white part and 2 inches of green part, chopped

2 tablespoons pine nuts

1 tablespoon toasted sesame seeds

Salt to taste

Freshly ground black pepper to taste

1 Heat the sesame oil in a large skillet or a wok.

2 Add the snow peas and scallions and sauté over medium heat, tossing frequently, for 3 minutes.

3 Add the remaining ingredients and cook an additional 3 minutes.

Makes 4 to 6 servings

HILLBILLY JIM'S COLLARD GREENS WITH SMOKED TURKEY

"**This former Federation Superstar** would rather eat collard greens and smoked turkey than romance a pretty lady, and this big ol' Kentuckian looooves pretty ladies! This is a southern staple that's actually quite healthy. Try it and you'll be yelling 'Yah-hoo' at the supper table."

3 cups water
½ pound smoked turkey, pre-cooked
   and cut into 1-inch pieces
1½ pounds collard greens
2 tablespoons vegetable oil
½ teaspoon salt
½ teaspoon coarsely ground black pepper
½ teaspoon sugar
½ teaspoon crushed red pepper flakes

1 In a 4-quart saucepan, bring the water and the turkey to a boil over high heat. Reduce heat and simmer, covered, for 45 minutes. Remove the turkey from the pot (reserve the liquid).

2 Wash the collard greens until all of the dirt has been removed.

3 Chop the greens into ½-inch pieces. Add them to the liquid in the saucepan, along with the oil, salt, pepper, sugar, and red pepper flakes. Bring the mixture to a boil, then reduce the heat and simmer, covered, for 30 minutes.

4 Drain the greens, add the turkey, and serve.

Makes 6 servings

HEADBANGERS' STUFFED 'SHROOMS

"**Okay, so your cardiologist** might not endorse this recipe, but you don't have to eat a pound of these rich mushrooms, do you? Remember: moderation. I somehow doubt that New Jersey's Headbangers make this appetizer on a regular basis, but it is a good one. Do you really think that Mosh and Thrasher actually own a serving tray? I didn't think so."

8 medium-size fresh button mushrooms

1 tablespoon butter or margarine

2 ounces cream cheese (low-fat, if desired)

½ tablespoon heavy cream or milk

½ teaspoon fresh minced chives

½ teaspoon fresh lemon juice

½ teaspoon salt

Freshly ground black pepper to taste

Paprika to taste

Parsley for garnish

1 Preheat the oven to 350 degrees.

2 Remove the mushroom stems and discard them. Wash the caps and dry them.

3 Put the butter in a shallow baking pan or casserole and place in the oven to melt.

4 In a small bowl, combine the cream cheese, cream, chives, lemon juice, salt, and pepper. Using a fork, mix until smooth.

Makes 4 servings

5 Spoon a generous amount of the mixture into each inverted mushroom cap and sprinkle lightly with paprika.

6 Place the mushroom caps in the baking dish and return it to the oven to bake for 10 to 15 minutes.

7 Place the mushrooms on a serving tray and garnish with the parsley. Serve with toothpicks.

MICHAEL COLE'S SWEET GLAZED BABY CARROTS

"My pal Michael came through with this gem. I have to say that Michael's carrots taste a whole lot better than his frosted hair looks. (Only a joke, folks.)"

1 (1-pound) package baby carrots
   (fresh or frozen)
2 tablespoons butter
1½ tablespoons brown sugar
Salt to taste
Freshly ground black pepper to taste

1 In a medium saucepan, bring the carrots to a boil, then cook on medium-high heat for 8 to 10 minutes, or until cooked but still firm. Drain the carrots and put them back in the pan.

2 Lower the heat and add the butter and brown sugar. Season with salt and pepper.

3 Cook for 5 to 10 minutes on low heat.

Makes 4 servings

CHYNA'S PICO DE GALLO

"**Why use store-bought** when you can make this Pico de Gallo from scratch and get a standing ovation? Chyna is considered one of the most complex performers in the World Wrestling Federation, but fortunately her dip is simple and quick to make. Be careful of the jalapeños, as they can have evil intentions."

8 jalapeño peppers, seeded
    and chopped, or to taste
2 medium tomatoes, chopped
1 white onion, peeled and chopped
3 cloves garlic, peeled and minced
½ cup fresh lemon juice
1 cup chopped fresh cilantro
Salt to taste
Freshly ground black pepper to taste

1 In a bowl, combine all the ingredients except salt and pepper and blend well.

2 Season with salt and pepper.

3 Eat with tortilla chips (baked chips have fewer calories than fried) or as a condiment.

Makes 4 servings

THE ROCK'S "SMACK-ARONI" SALAD

"**The Rock eats his share** of carbs in the form of macaroni at least five days a week, and almost always before 4 P.M. This recipe is '*WrestleMania* level' and keeps well in the fridge. Please try it, it's one of my all-time favorites. My friend Joe at the Central Deli in Darien, Connecticut, makes it every day."

1 (1-pound) package elbow macaroni

1 carrot, shredded

3 stalks celery, chopped fine

½ medium onion, chopped fine

2 tablespoons mayonnaise

1 Cook the pasta, strain it, and run cold water over it until cold. Cool in the refrigerator for about 2 hours.

2 In a large mixing bowl, stir together the cold pasta with the carrot, celery, and onion, mixing thoroughly. Add the mayonnaise and stir until well blended. Refrigerate before serving.

Makes 8 to 10 servings

RIKISHI'S RICE CASSEROLE WITH BROCCOLI

"**Even though his backside** has more dimples than a Titleist golf ball, Rikishi has used his most prominent asset to gain fame as a wrestler. This giant Samoan and his ample backside have become one of the hottest acts in the World Wrestling Federation. Go figure. Rikishi's Samoan heritage brings with it a love for rice in a variety of dishes, and Mrs. Rikishi says her husband can really put away large quantities of this family favorite."

¼ cup chopped onions

1 tablespoon margarine

⅓ cup milk

¾ cup cubed low-fat Velveeta cheese

2 cups cooked rice, drained

1 (8-ounce) package frozen broccoli, chopped (or use fresh)

1 (10.5-ounce) can cream of chicken soup

½ teaspoon salt

1 Preheat the oven to 350 degrees.

2 Cook the onions in the margarine until soft and translucent.

3 Add them to the remaining ingredients and mix gently.

4 Bake in a 2-quart baking dish for 1 hour, until the top is golden.

Makes 4 servings

J.R.'S GREEN BEAN CASSEROLE

"**I must have been** eight or ten years old when Mom first made this. I'm not sure where she got the recipe, and when Dad and I looked at it for the first time, we were a little leery. We didn't recognize what we were about to eat, but we sure didn't want to upset Mom, so we dug in. We were men and it was our duty to eat whatever was put in front of us. To our surprise, it was good . . . very good . . . so good it became a fixture around the Ross home."

1 (10.5-ounce) can cream of
    mushroom soup
½ cup milk
1 teaspoon soy sauce (optional)
3 dashes freshly ground black pepper
4 cups cooked French-cut green beans
1⅓ cups canned French-fried onions

1 Preheat the oven to 350 degrees.

2 Mix the soup, milk, soy sauce, pepper, green beans, and ⅔ cup of the onions in a 1½-quart casserole dish.

3 Bake for 25 minutes, or until hot throughout.

4 Stir the casserole, then sprinkle the remaining ⅔ cup onions on the top.

5 Bake another 5 minutes, or until the onions are browned.

Makes 6 servings

"**Lita made very little money** early in her career, and she mastered this economical yet sassy dish while living in Mexico City. This dish was rumored to be on the catering table during the filming of Mel Brooks's classic film *Blazing Saddles.* True or not, take it from me, this one is a winner. Like Lita, this dish is sassy . . . and unforgettable."

¼ pound bacon, chopped

1 large onion, peeled and chopped

2 large garlic cloves, peeled and chopped

2½ tablespoons chili powder

1 (4-ounce) can diced green chilies

2 (15- to 16-ounce) cans black beans, drained and rinsed

2 teaspoons dried oregano

¼ teaspoon cayenne pepper

1 (16-ounce) can diced, peeled tomatoes, undrained

Salt to taste

Freshly ground black pepper to taste

1 Cook the bacon in a large, heavy saucepan over medium heat until light brown, about 10 minutes.

2 Add the onion and garlic and sauté until the onion is translucent, about 5 minutes.

3 Add all the remaining ingredients. Simmer until the mixture is thick, stirring frequently, about 12 minutes.

4 Season with salt and pepper.

Makes 4 servings

TEST'S TOSTADOS WITH CHICKEN AND BLACK BEAN GUACAMOLE

"If you are craving good Mexican food and don't feel like going out, this recipe really delivers. I can just see Test, a smooth operator, whipping this one up for one of his lady friends."

1 large, ripe avocado, pitted and peeled

4 teaspoons fresh lime juice, plus more to taste

⅔ cup rinsed, drained canned black beans

2 scallions, white and green parts, chopped

Hot pepper sauce (such as Tabasco) to taste

Salt to taste

Freshly ground black pepper to taste

2 cooked chicken breasts, shredded

1 tomato, seeded and chopped

3 tablespoons chopped fresh cilantro

1 teaspoon ground cumin

4 tostado shells (crisp corn tortillas)

2 cups shredded lettuce

⅔ cup crumbled mild goat or feta cheese

Fresh salsa to taste

1 Place the avocado in a medium bowl. Add 4 teaspoons of the lime juice and mash until almost smooth. Mix in the beans and scallions. Season the guacamole to taste with hot sauce, salt, and pepper.

2 In a small bowl, combine the shredded chicken, tomato, cilantro, and cumin. Season the chicken mixture to taste with lime juice, salt, and pepper.

3 Place the tostado shells on 4 plates. Layer in the lettuce, guacamole, and chicken mixture. Sprinkle with cheese and spoon on some salsa.

Makes 4 servings

TERRI'S SHRIMP AND AVOCADO SALAD

"**Terri? Shrimp?** Probably only a coincidence, but this recipe is actually one of Terri's favorites. I like the part where she instructs you to use *exactly* eighteen cherry or grape tomatoes. Try this little dish and think of the petite she-devil."

1 small avocado, pitted, peeled, and chopped

½ cup buttermilk

1 (3-ounce) package cream cheese (reduced-fat, if desired)

1 tablespoon fresh lemon juice

1 small clove garlic, peeled

¼ teaspoon hot pepper sauce, such as Tabasco

¼ teaspoon salt

6 cups torn lettuce

1 pound small shrimp, peeled, deveined, and steamed

18 cherry or grape tomatoes, halved

4 ounces low-fat Swiss cheese, cut into julienne strips

Freshly ground black pepper to taste

1 Place the first 7 ingredients in a blender and blend until smooth.

2 Arrange the lettuce in a salad bowl, then place the shrimp, tomatoes, and cheese on top.

3 Sprinkle with a little pepper and toss with the avocado mixture.

Makes 6 servings

ACOLYTES' BEER BREAD

"**Cut off my legs** and call me Shorty if this isn't the easiest home-made bread recipe you've ever seen! Can't you just imagine Bradshaw and Faarooq with matching pastel aprons in the kitchen making fresh bread for the boys at the weekly poker game? Very touching."

3 cups self-rising flour
1 tablespoon sugar
1 six-pack beer
1 tablespoon butter, melted

1 Preheat the oven to 325 degrees.

2 In a large bowl, blend the flour and sugar. Quickly mix in one can of beer. Put the mixture into a greased 9 × 5-inch loaf pan. Wet your fingers, and smooth the top.

3 Bake for 1 hour, or until golden brown.

4 Drink the other 5 beers while you're waiting.

5 Brush the top of the bread with melted butter.

Makes 6 servings

TAZZ'S RED HOOK GARLIC BREAD

"**Growing up Italian** in the Red Hook section of Brooklyn, one of the Big Apple's toughest neighborhoods, the controversial Tazz loved his mom's wonderful garlic bread, but he was reluctant to share this family treasure with us. And guys, don't use stale bread. Get off the couch, go to the store, and get fresh bread. You'll be very happy you did."

½ cup (1 stick) butter, melted

4 garlic cloves, peeled and minced
(or 1 tablespoon minced garlic in a jar)

1 (1-pound) unsliced French bread
baguette, halved lengthwise

4 tablespoons grated Parmesan cheese

Paprika to taste

Freshly ground black pepper to taste

1 Preheat the broiler.

2 Combine the butter and garlic.

3 Place the bread on a baking sheet and brush each cut side with the garlic-butter mixture. Sprinkle each half with 2 tablespoons of the Parmesan cheese and season with paprika and pepper.

4 Broil about 5 minutes until golden brown. Cut into 1-inch-wide slices and serve immediately.

Makes 6 servings

"When Steven provided this banana nut bread recipe, I thought, How appropriate. Steven's TV personality is very nutty, to say the least. But this recipe is a surefire main-event hit! Young Steven is still finding himself, as we say in the business, but this nut bread is all the way there. Take my advice and enjoy it with a glass of ice-cold milk."

¼ cup plus 1 tablespoon sour cream

1 teaspoon baking soda

½ cup (1 stick) butter, at room temperature

1 cup sugar

2 eggs

1 cup mashed ripe banana (about 2 bananas)

2 cups flour

½ teaspoon baking powder

1 cup chopped walnuts or pecans

1 Preheat the oven to 350 degrees.

2 Grease a 9 × 5-inch loaf pan.

3 In a small bowl, combine the sour cream and baking soda.

4 In a large bowl, cream the butter and sugar with an electric mixer. Beat in the eggs, bananas, and sour cream mixture. Sift in the flour and baking powder, stir to blend, then stir in the nuts.

5 Spoon the mixture into the pan and bake about 1 hour, until a toothpick inserted into the center comes out clean and the loaf is golden brown.

6 Cool for 10 minutes in the pan. Turn the loaf out onto a rack and let cool completely.

Makes 6 to 8 servings

STEVEN RICHARDS'S "UNCENSORED" BANANA NUT BREAD

J.R. 'S MAMA'S PERFECT ROLLS

"**I think these rolls** were the primary reason my britches were from the husky section of the Sears boys department. Yes, these rolls taste great, but the aroma they give off while they're baking is pure heaven. This was a family staple at Christmas, Thanksgiving, and special Sunday dinners. Mama's gone, but her memory lives on with these perfect rolls."

1 (¼-ounce) package dry yeast

2 cups lukewarm water

¾ cup sugar

¾ cup cooking oil

5 cups self-rising flour

1 Dissolve the yeast in the warm water. Add the sugar and oil, then stir in the flour.

2 Place the dough in a glass bowl and cover. Refrigerate overnight.

3 Form the dough into 2-inch balls and place on a greased baking sheet 2 inches apart. Cover and set them aside for 2 hours to let them rise.

4 Preheat the oven to 400 degrees.

5 Bake for 15 minutes, or until golden.

Makes 12 rolls

Note: This recipe may also be used for cinnamon rolls. Just add cinnamon and sugar to taste and roll the balls in the mixture before baking.

J.R.'S COUNTRY CORN BREAD

"If you wanted to have successful dates as a young man in rural Oklahoma, you had to like corn bread. Almost every young lady's mom took pride in made-from-scratch corn bread and had a big plateful at every important meal. You knew you were in business when your date's dad invited you to join him for dessert—corn bread crumbled up in ice-cold milk! Ah, things were so much simpler back then."

1½ cups cornmeal

½ cup sugar (optional)

½ cup flour

4 teaspoons baking powder

½ teaspoon salt

1½ cups milk

1 egg, beaten

½ cup oil or melted shortening

1 Preheat the oven to 425 degrees.

2 In a large bowl, mix together the cornmeal, sugar (if desired), flour, baking powder, and salt.

3 Add the milk, egg, and oil, stirring only enough to mix well.

4 Pour the mixture into a 9-inch square baking dish or casserole and bake until the bread is light brown, about 25 minutes, or until a toothpick inserted in the center comes out clean.

Makes about 6 servings

Note: Double the recipe for a 13 × 9-inch pan.

J.R. says, "Bakes even better in a cast-iron skillet."

FINISHING MANEUVER

Desserts

KANE'S RED VELVET CAKE

"**Like Kane,** this recipe is a little complex. And like Kane, the finished product is a work of art. You've got to be in the baking mood, but it is well worth the effort. Kane is one of the Federation's biggest and most powerful stars, and this cake, like the big red machine, is stronger than a government mule."

CAKE:

1 (10¼-ounce) package fudge
    marble cake mix

1 teaspoon baking soda

2 eggs

1½ cups buttermilk

1 (1-ounce) bottle red food coloring

FROSTING:

5 tablespoons flour

1 cup milk

1 cup (2 sticks) butter or margarine, softened

1 cup sugar

2 teaspoons vanilla

1 Preheat the oven to 350 degrees.

2 To make the cake, in a large bowl, combine the cake mix and baking soda. Add the eggs, buttermilk, and food coloring. With a beater, blend on low until moistened, then beat on high for 2 minutes.

3 Pour the batter into 2 greased and floured 9-inch cake pans and bake for 30 to 35 minutes, or until a toothpick inserted into the center comes out clean.

4 Let cool for 10 minutes. Remove the cakes from the pans to a wire rack to let cool completely.

5 To make the frosting, whisk the flour and milk in a saucepan over medium-low heat until smooth. Bring to a boil. Whisk and stir for 2 more minutes, or until the sauce has thickened. Cover the mixture and refrigerate.

6 In a mixing bowl, cream the butter and sugar. Add the chilled milk mixture and beat until fluffy, about 10 minutes. Stir in the vanilla.

7 Frost the top of one of the cake layers. Carefully place the second layer on top of the first. Frost the sides of the cake and then the top.

Makes 6 to 8 servings

Optional: You may prefer to use Betty Crocker's soft whipped vanilla icing. Delicious and easy!

CLASSY FREDDY BLASSIE'S "CLASSY" CHEESECAKE

"**Freddy Blassie** is an American original—a true legend within the wrestling fraternity. Watch the movie *Breakfast with Blassie* with Andy Kaufman and you'll die laughing. Freddy has long been a dessert man, and he apparently picked up this delicious cheesecake recipe during one of his many world travels."

CRUST:

> 1 cup graham cracker crumbs
>
> ¼ cup coarsely chopped walnuts
>
> 2 tablespoons brown sugar
>
> 1 teaspoon ground cinnamon
>
> ½ cup (1 stick) unsalted butter, softened

FILLING:

> 2 cups sour cream
>
> 3 (8-ounce) packages cream cheese, at room temperature
>
> 3 eggs, lightly beaten
>
> 1 cup granulated sugar
>
> ½ teaspoon salt
>
> 2 teaspoons pure vanilla extract
>
> Zest of 1 small orange, finely grated

1 Preheat the oven to 375 degrees.

2 To make the crust, combine the graham cracker crumbs, walnuts, brown sugar, and cinnamon. Add the butter and toss to combine.

3 Reserve 3 tablespoons of the graham cracker mixture for the top of the cheesecake and press the rest evenly across the bottom, and 1½ inches up the side, of a 9-inch pie pan.

4 To make the filling, blend the sour cream, cream cheese, eggs, granulated sugar, and salt in a food processor or blender until very smooth. Add the vanilla and orange zest and process just enough to blend.

5 Add the filling to the piecrust and bake for 50 minutes.

6 Sprinkle the reserved topping over the cake and bake until the filling is firm and the top is lightly golden, 10 to 15 minutes more.

7 Cool completely and refrigerate until chilled.

Makes 6 to 8 servings

MARK HENRY'S "SEXUAL CHOCOLATE" CAKE

"**The 1996 Olympic weight lifter** Mark Henry is one of the most charismatic athletes in the World Wrestling Federation, but he has 'issues with food.' In other words, the jovial Texan prefers to use the low-fat tips when baking this tasty cake. Mark's toughest opponent may well be his weight, and if he is victorious, the World's Strongest Man could be a major force in the Federation."

1 package devil's food cake mix

1 (12-ounce) can Eagle Brand sweetened condensed milk

1 (8-ounce) jar caramel ice cream topping

1 (8-ounce) carton Cool Whip

3 Skor or Heath candy bars, crumbled

1 Mix and bake the cake according to the directions on the package.

2 Perforate the cake with a fork or a toothpick. Pour the can of milk over the cake.

3 Top with the caramel topping and cover with Cool Whip. Sprinkle with the candy bars and serve.

LOW-FAT TIPS:

✘ Use fat-free Eagle milk.

✘ Use fat-free Cool Whip.

✘ Use Smuckers fat-free caramel topping.

✘ Use Sweet Rewards devil's food cake mix.

Makes 8 servings

ALBERT'S APPLESAUCE CAKE

"Old 8⅜ comes through big time with this Applesauce Cake. Multiple-pierced Albert wore a 8⅜-inch football helmet at Pittsburgh, where he started three years as an offensive lineman. The 6-foot 7-inch 330-pounder loves children, has a degree in education from the University of Pittsburgh, and has worked extensively with kids with learning disabilities. I feel this youngster is going to be a top hand in the Federation because of his size, intelligence, and work ethic. If you use Mott's applesauce (it's the best), you'll really love the results."

2 cups sugar

½ cup (1 stick) butter

3½ cups flour

1 teaspoon ground cloves

1 teaspoon ground cinnamon

1 teaspoon ground nutmeg

1 teaspoon ground ginger

½ teaspoon salt

3 cups applesauce

4 teaspoons baking soda

1 cup raisins

1 cup chopped nuts

1 cup chopped dates

1 Preheat the oven to 375 degrees. Grease and flour a 10-inch tube pan or two 9 × 5-inch loaf pans.

2 Cream the sugar and butter. Sift 3 cups of the flour with the cloves, cinnamon, nutmeg, ginger, and salt, and add the mixture to the sugar and butter.

3 Add the applesauce and mix in the baking soda. Mix the remaining ½ cup of flour with the raisins, nuts, and dates, and add to the applesauce batter.

4 Pour the batter into the prepared pan(s). Bake for 1 hour, or until a toothpick inserted into the center comes out clean.

Makes 4 to 6 servings

GERALD BRISCO'S "BEST CAKE EVER"

"**I don't know about the title** of this little dandy, but let me tell you, folks, it's *real* good. Gerald Brisco, a Native American of Choctaw and Chickasaw descent from Blackwell, Oklahoma, has recently lost about fifty pounds following a low-carb diet and taking about one hundred vitamins and supplements a day! He misses his favorite cake, but I hear that he cheats now and then, falling off the wagon long enough for a healthy-sized piece. And he can eat all the cake he wants if he promises never to appear on TV in drag again! (The sight of Gerald in a dress almost drove his legendary brother Jack Brisco into seclusion.)"

2 boxes Duncan Hines cake mix, butter recipe

2 (14-ounce) cans crushed pineapple, undrained

2 cups sugar

2 (5-ounce) boxes vanilla pudding and pie filling (not instant)

1 (8-ounce) container plus 1 (12-ounce) container Cool Whip

2 cups shredded coconut

1 Bake the two cakes following the directions on the box for 13 × 9 × 2-inch pans.

2 Combine the cans of pineapple with the sugar in a medium saucepan and boil for 5 minutes.

3 Cook the pudding following the directions on the package.

4 Poke holes with a fork in the top of one cake and spread half of the pineapple sauce over the top and sides. Spread ½ inch of the vanilla pudding over the pineapple sauce.

5 Place the second cake on top of the first, and add the remaining pineapple
sauce and pudding to the top and sides. Cover with Cool Whip.

6 Lightly toast the coconut in a 350-degree oven for 10 minutes, or until golden,
and sprinkle it over the top and sides of the cake.

7 Refrigerate, then eat—and watch the scales!

Makes 12 servings

MANKIND'S PUMPKIN PIE

"**Mick and I** have been known to enjoy the occasional piece of pie. It's hard to believe, he and I being the physical marvels that we are, but it's true. A little-known fact: Mick and I are actually considered the resident pie experts in the World Wrestling Federation. We highly recommend this pie, which makes its excellence official."

¾ **cup sugar**

½ **teaspoon salt**

1 **teaspoon ground cinnamon**

2 **eggs**

1 **(12-ounce) can low-fat evaporated milk**

1 **(15-ounce) can Libby's pumpkin filling**

1 **Pillsbury piecrust**

Low-fat Cool Whip or light whipped topping to taste

1 Preheat the oven to 425 degrees.

2 Combine the sugar, salt, and cinnamon in a small bowl.

3 In a large bowl, beat the eggs lightly, then stir in the sugar mixture. Gradually stir in the evaporated milk and canned pumpkin.

4 Place the piecrust into a 9-inch pie pan and pour in the pumpkin mixture.

5 Bake for 15 minutes, then reduce the temperature to 350 degrees and bake for 40 to 50 minutes, or until a knife inserted into the center comes out clean.

6 Cool on a wire rack for 2 hours. Serve immediately or chill. Do not freeze.

7 Top with Cool Whip and serve.

Makes 6 to 8 servings

KURT ANGLE'S ALL-AMERICAN APPLE PIE

"**It's true, it's true . . .** this may be the best apple pie you've ever tasted! Kurt Angle may soon be your favorite World Wrestling Federation Superstar, and this will, no doubt, become your favorite apple pie. Kurt grew up in Pittsburgh, and his mom baked for her boys, who usually put away two of these delights in one sitting. Try the pie. Enough said."

1 cup sugar

2 tablespoons flour

1 teaspoon ground cinnamon

Dash of ground nutmeg

6 cups peeled, cored, and thinly sliced cooking apples (assorted: Granny Smith, Red or Golden Delicious, for example)

1 package Pillsbury ready-made piecrust

1 tablespoon butter

1 Preheat the oven to 425 degrees.

2 Combine the sugar, flour, cinnamon, and nutmeg.

3 Add the sugar mixture to the sliced apples and toss to coat the fruit.

4 Line a 9-inch pie plate with the piecrust, and fill it with the apple mixture. Dot the mixture with butter.

5 Add the top crust and pinch the edges.

6 Cover the edge of the pie with foil and bake for 40 to 45 minutes.

Makes 6 to 8 servings

"**I seriously doubt** that Mr. McMahon has ever rolled up his sleeves and sauntered, chest out, into the kitchen to make McMahon Millionaire Pie. However, this is a family favorite, and rumor has it Mr. McMahon once fired a chef for not using Eagle Brand milk."

McMAHON MILLIONAIRE PIE

1 cup coconut

1 cup crushed pineapple, undrained

1 cup chopped pecans

½ cup sugar

1 (12-ounce) can Eagle Brand sweetened condensed milk

1 (12-ounce) carton Cool Whip

½ cup lemon juice

1 premade graham cracker crust

1 Mix together all the ingredients except the crust and pour them into the graham cracker crust.

2 Cover with wax paper and chill for 1 hour or overnight.

Makes 8 servings

"**I've heard that X-Pac's mom** used to make this one when he was a youngster to try to fatten him up. It's his favorite, and he's one of mine. I can even vouch for this recipe because I've made it myself, so I know anyone can do it. We never had air-conditioning at our house in the Sooner State, so on hot summer days Mom was always looking for good things to fix for dinner that wouldn't warm up the kitchen. Not much heat used in this recipe, and having taken the oath, I can attest that this is a great pie."

1 (3-ounce) package vanilla pie and pudding mix (not instant)

1 (3-ounce) package banana cream pudding mix (not instant)

3½ cups milk (use 2% for less fat)

1 large ripe banana

1 premade chocolate graham cracker crust

Light Cool Whip or light whipped topping to taste

X-PAC'S BANANA CREAM PIE

1 In a medium saucepan, combine both the vanilla and the banana cream pie mixes with the milk. Bring the mixture to a light boil over medium-low heat, then cool for 10 minutes.

2 Cut the banana into ¼-inch slices and place them on the bottom of the chocolate piecrust. Add the pudding mixture.

3 Refrigerate for 4 to 5 hours. Top with Cool Whip and serve.

Makes 6 servings

THE GODFATHER'S "MAKIN' CHOCOLATE PIE IS EASY" RECIPE

"**The 6-foot 8-inch** former All-American high school basketball player keeps it real . . . and simple. Even your family's slow cousin can cook like Emeril Lagasse with this foolproof dessert recipe."

2 (3-ounce) packages Jell-O
   instant chocolate pudding

1½ cups milk

3½ cups thawed low-fat Cool Whip

1 premade chocolate graham
   cracker crust

1 Mix the Jell-O and milk and stir in the Cool Whip.

2 Spoon the mixture into the graham cracker crust.

3 Chill for 2 hours and serve.

**Makes
8 servings**

BROTHER LOVE'S HEAVENLY FUDGE SQUARES

"**Longtime World Wrestling Federation** fans remember the controversial and portly Brother Love for his outrageous interviews with Federation Superstars and his patented phrase, 'I *LOVE* YOU!' Brother Love had a sweet tooth as pronounced as his colorful character and, the legend goes, could put away his favorite fudge in mass quantities with the proper motivation—he had to be awake! When you're in the mood for serious fudge, try this one on for size. By the way, Brother Love is actually Houston, Texas, native Bruce Prichard, and he now coordinates the Federation's Talent Development Program."

FOR THE FUDGE SQUARES:

½ cup margarine or butter

1½ squares unsweetened chocolate

1¾ cups graham cracker crumbs

1 cup flaked coconut

½ cup chopped pecans

¼ cup sugar

2 tablespoons water

1 teaspoon vanilla

FOR THE TOPPING:

2 cups powdered sugar

¼ cup margarine or butter, softened

2 tablespoons milk

1 teaspoon vanilla

1½ squares unsweetened chocolate

1 To make the fudge squares, line a 9 × 9-inch square pan with aluminum foil, allowing the foil to come over the sides of the pan.

2 Over low heat in a 3-quart saucepan, melt the margarine and chocolate, stirring occasionally. Remove from the heat.

3 Stir in the graham cracker crumbs, coconut, pecans, sugar, water, and vanilla. Press the mixture into the pan and refrigerate.

4 To make the topping, in a bowl, mix together the powdered sugar, margarine, milk, and vanilla. Spread over the fudge. Refrigerate for 15 minutes.

5 In a small saucepan over low heat, melt the chocolate. Drizzle over the top of the fudge. Refrigerate for 2 hours, or until hardened.

6 Using the foil, lift the fudge from the pan. Fold the foil back to cut the squares. Cover and refrigerate leftover squares.

Makes 25 squares

"These cookies are eyebrow-raisin', people's elbow—droppin' delicious! Strikes me as funny that there may be some among us who think that by eating the Rock's favorite chocolate chip cookies, they will look like The Great One. That just don't work. I tried it. But these are *WrestleMania*-level cookies . . . and best enjoyed with ice-cold milk."

1 cup (2 sticks) butter, at room temperature

1 cup granulated sugar

1 cup brown sugar

2 eggs

1 teaspoon vanilla

2 cups flour

2½ cups quick oatmeal, blended to a fine powder in a food processor or blender

½ teaspoon salt

1 teaspoon baking powder

1 teaspoon baking soda

12 ounces chocolate chips

½ 8-ounce Hershey bar, grated

1½ cups chopped nuts (walnuts, pecans, or mixture)

1 Preheat the oven to 375 degrees.

2 Cream the butter, granulated sugar, and brown sugar. Stir in the eggs and vanilla. Blend in the flour, oatmeal, salt, baking powder, and baking soda. Add the chocolate chips, Hershey bar, and nuts.

3 Roll the dough into ¾- to 1-inch-wide balls and place them 2 inches apart on a lightly greased cookie sheet.

4 Bake 10 minutes, or until browned to suit.

Makes 4 to 5 dozen cookies

THE HOLLYS' FAMILY BUTTER COOKIES

"**Whether or not the Hollys** are actually cousins isn't important. It also doesn't matter that Crash looks and sounds like cartoon legend Elroy Jetson, and Hardcore Holly is one of the toughest guys in the World Wrestling Federation. What does matter is that these cookies are absolutely delicious and easy to make—even if you've never baked anything in your life."

2 cups (4 sticks) butter
2 cups sugar
6 eggs
2 teaspoons vanilla
8 cups flour
4 teaspoons baking powder

1 Preheat the oven to 375 degrees.

2 Cream the butter and sugar in a large bowl. Beat the eggs into the mixture and add the vanilla. Stir in the flour and baking powder.

3 Push the dough through a cookie press or roll it on a lightly floured board and cut it into shapes of your choice.

4 Bake on a greased cookie sheet until the cookies are lightly brown, 5 to 10 minutes.

Makes about 8 dozen cookies

VISCERA'S NO-BAKE COOKIES

"**Quite honestly,** we don't encourage Big Vis to put away a lot of cookies. We'd like to see his weight under 500 pounds, as we don't want to adversely affect his dropkicks. But even Vis needs a treat every now and then, and who's gonna tell him to put down the cookies?"

½ cup (1 stick) butter

2 cups sugar

½ cup milk

4 tablespoons unsweetened cocoa powder

2 cups oatmeal

½ cup peanut butter

1 teaspoon vanilla

1 Combine the butter, sugar, milk, and cocoa in a saucepan. Boil the mixture for 1 minute.

2 Remove the pan from the stove, and add the oatmeal, peanut butter, and vanilla.

3 Form the mixture into balls and drop them onto wax paper.

4 Cool and serve.

Makes 2 to 3 dozen cookies

PERRY SATURN'S SUPER COOKIES

"**I'm not sure** if Saturn learned this simple super cookie recipe when he was in the U.S. Army Rangers or if his tattoo artist suggested it to him one long afternoon in the chair. Needless to say, this recipe is virtually foolproof and can make a great last-minute dessert for those uninvited, just-happened-to-be-in-the-neighborhood guests."

1 box cake mix (any flavor)
1 egg
⅓ cup oil

1 Preheat the oven to 350 degrees.

2 Mix all the ingredients well.

3 Drop teaspoonfuls of the dough onto a greased cookie sheet and bake for 8 to 10 minutes, or until golden.

Makes 3 dozen cookies

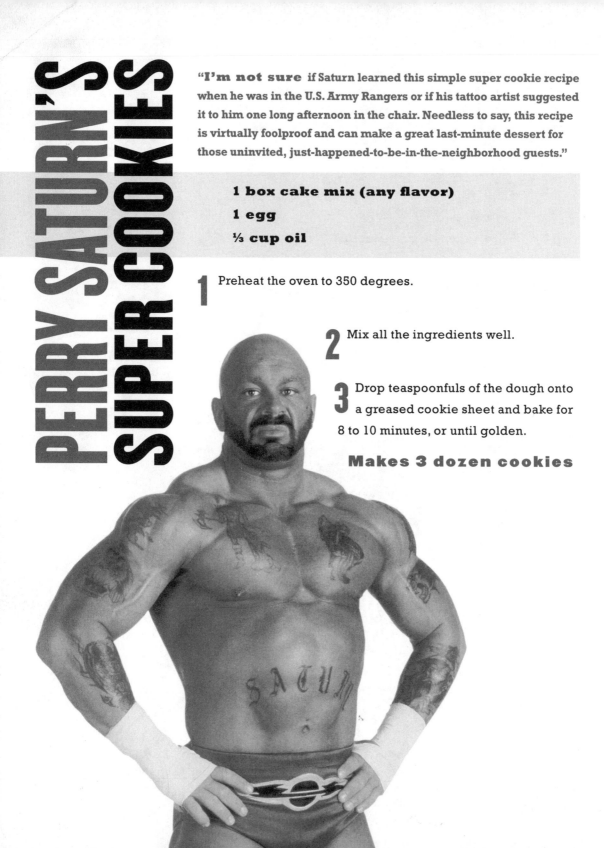

ROAD DOGG'S OATMEAL COOKIES

"**In the name of good health,** you should regularly consume several of the Road Dogg's Oatmeal Cookies. Great source of fiber, you see. The Road Dogg, a former marine and veteran of the Gulf War, has three older brothers—all wrestlers—so the competition for the last cookie of the batch escalated as the boys grew older and bigger. Nothing makes a southern mama prouder than to see her boys in a fistfight over her cookies."

1 cup flour

½ teaspoon baking powder

½ teaspoon baking soda

¼ teaspoon salt

¼ cup shortening

4 tablespoons (½ stick) butter or margarine

½ cup granulated sugar, plus more for dipping (optional)

⅓ cup packed brown sugar

1 egg

2 tablespoons milk

½ teaspoon vanilla

1 cup quick-cooking rolled oats

¼ cup chopped walnuts

1 Preheat the oven to 375 degrees.

2 In a small bowl, stir together the flour, baking powder, baking soda, and salt.

3 In a mixer bowl, beat the shortening and butter for 30 seconds. Add the granulated sugar and brown sugar and beat until fluffy. Add the egg, milk, and vanilla, and beat well.

4 Add the flour mixture to the butter mixture, beating until well combined. Stir in the oats and walnuts.

5 Chill the dough for 2 hours, then form it into 1-inch balls. Dip the tops of the balls into granulated sugar, if desired.

6 Place the balls on a greased cookie sheet, and bake for 10 to 12 minutes, until baked through but *not* golden.

Makes 3 dozen cookies

BIG BOSS MAN'S REFRIGERATED DOUGH COOKIES

"The Boss Man knows his dough— the edible kind and, believe it or not, the bankable kind. This big country boy is a shrewd businessman who has relied on common sense and instinct to make several very profitable real estate deals down in Georgia. He's also the father of two beautiful little girls and very active in nonprofit organizations in his community."

1 or 2 packages of ready-made cookie dough (in your store's refrigerator case)

1 Cut the dough into slices.

2 Place the slices on a cookie sheet sprayed with nonstick cooking spray.

3 Follow directions on the package for times and oven heat.

4 Enjoy!

Makes 2 to 4 dozen cookies

"**The Hardy Boyz** really are brothers, and they may end their careers as the most spectacular tag team in Federation history. No one creates a greater aerial offense than these two, and you can create some excitement of your own with this very healthful dessert."

1 pint ripe strawberries, hulled and quartered

1 pint ripe blueberries

¼ cup granulated sugar

2 teaspoons brown sugar

¼ teaspoon vanilla extract

2 teaspoons lemon extract

1 Entenmann's fat-free Golden Loaf, or your favorite low-fat brand

1 (8-ounce) container low-fat Cool Whip

1 Reserve a few berries for garnish. Combine the berries, granulated sugar, brown sugar, vanilla, and lemon extract and stir until the sugars dissolve. Let the mixture sit for 30 minutes, then refrigerate it for 2 hours.

2 Slice the loaf and spoon the berry mixture over it. Add a dollop or two of Cool Whip and top with one of the reserved berries.

Makes 6 servings

JERICHO DOODLES

"DOODLES ARE JERICHO!"

"Doodles Are Jericho? Someone is watching too much TV! But seriously, friends, these are big time! Like young Y2J, these are main-event every time out. Jericho Doodles get a huge tip of the hat from good old J.R."

3¾ cups flour

½ teaspoon baking soda

½ teaspoon salt

½ teaspoon cream of tartar

1 cup (2 sticks) butter

2 cups plus 3 tablespoons sugar

2 eggs

¼ cup milk

1 teaspoon vanilla

1 teaspoon ground cinnamon

1 Preheat the oven to 375 degrees.

2 Grease a cookie sheet.

3 In a medium bowl, stir together the flour, baking soda, salt, and cream of tartar.

4 In another bowl, beat the butter for 30 seconds, then add 2 cups of the sugar and beat until fluffy. Add the eggs, milk, and vanilla. Beat well. Add the dry ingredients to the beaten mixture, beating until well combined.

5 With a teaspoon, shape the dough into 1-inch balls. Mix the remaining 3 tablespoons sugar with the cinnamon and roll the balls in the mixture to coat them. Flatten the balls slightly with the back of a spoon.

6 Place the balls on the cookie sheet and bake 8 minutes, or until light golden. Remove immediately.

Makes 6 dozen cookies

"Oh, Mama! Put the kids to bed and get in here! How, I ask you, can it get any better? This ice cream makes even Stone Cold smile, and yes, you can't sit still and eat it. To make this a *WrestleMania*-level dessert, use Cinnabon cinnamon."

> **3 cups heavy cream or whipping cream**
>
> **1 cup milk**
>
> **¾ cup sugar**
>
> **1 large vanilla bean (6 inches long),**
> **   halved lengthwise**
>
> **2 teaspoons ground cinnamon**
>
> **4 egg yolks**
>
> **Cinnamon sticks (optional)**

1 Combine the cream, milk, sugar, vanilla bean, and ground cinnamon in a heavy saucepan and cook over medium-low heat, stirring occasionally, until the sugar has dissolved and the mixture is hot, but don't let it come to a boil. Remove the pan from the heat. Remove the vanilla bean and scrape the seeds from the bean back into the cream mixture.

2 Whisk the egg yolks in a small bowl and slowly add 1 cup of the hot cream mixture, whisking constantly until smooth. Slowly pour the egg mixture back into the remaining cream mixture, whisking constantly.

3 Place the saucepan over medium heat and stir constantly until the mixture thickens, 10 to 15 minutes. Do not let the mixture come to a boil. Pour through a fine-mesh strainer into a bowl. Allow the custard to cool to room temperature, then refrigerate, loosely covered, for 2 hours.

4 Pour the chilled custard into the bowl of an ice cream maker and freeze according to the manufacturer's directions.

5 Place a cinnamon stick on top of each scoop for garnish, if desired.

Makes 1 quart

DEBRA'S MERLOT SORBET

"**Debra loves a nice glass** of Merlot every now and then, and this recipe from the blond beauty is magnificent. This sorbet is for adults only. Sorry, kids."

3 cups water
1½ cups sugar
1¼ cups Merlot

1 Combine the water and sugar in a saucepan and heat to a simmer. Cover and simmer for 5 minutes.

2 Stir in the wine and set the mixture aside to cool to room temperature. Refrigerate it, loosely covered, until chilled, 2 to 3 hours.

3 Freeze in an ice cream maker according to the manufacturer's directions.

4 Great served with fresh raspberries, blackberries, and blueberries.

Note: If you don't have an ice cream maker, put the mixture in a shallow pan and place it in the freezer for 4 to 5 hours, checking the consistency and stirring once every hour until smooth. When slushlike, transfer it to a serving bowl and refrigerate for 30 minutes.

Makes 5 cups

"**Some may say** that Mr. Backlund is three or four eggs short of a dozen, and I suppose they might be right. Well, this somewhat healthful dish uses a couple of eggs to create a unique-tasting ice cream. Add fresh fruit to give it a little personality, if you choose. Yes, Mr. Backlund may be as goofy as a pet coon, but he is also one of the nicest, most genuine guys in the business."

6 egg yolks

4 cups whole milk

1 cup Equal Spoonful sweetener

½ teaspoon salt

4 cups heavy cream

2 tablespoons vanilla extract

1 Beat the egg yolks and pour them into a 3-quart saucepan. Stir in the milk, Equal Spoonful, and salt. Stirring constantly with a wooden spoon, cook over low heat until the mixture lightly coats the back of the spoon, about 15 minutes.

2 Remove the pan from the heat and allow the mixture to cool for about 10 minutes. Stir in the cream and vanilla. Chill the mixture in the freezer for about 15 minutes.

3 Pour the mixture into an electric or manual ice cream maker and process according to the manufacturer's directions.

Makes 2 quarts

BOB BACKLUND'S LOW-CARB VANILLA ICE CREAM

STEPHANIE'S TASTY GREENWICH APPLES

"**Legend has it that** Stephanie's fourth nanny introduced this treat to the little princess. Even though seedless grapes were plentiful, Stephanie used to insist that her farsighted nanny manually remove the seeds from a seeded variety just for her own amusement. Not surprisingly, that unemployed nanny now reportedly refuses to eat grapes in any form. Even jelly! How sad."

2 medium Golden Delicious apples, unpeeled, cored, and cut into chunks

1 (8-ounce) can unsweetened pineapple chunks, undrained

½ cup seedless grapes

½ cup orange juice

½ teaspoon ground cinnamon

1 tablespoon butter, cut into pieces

1 Preheat the oven to 350 degrees.

2 In a 9 × 11-inch baking dish, combine the apples, pineapple chunks and juice, and grapes. Drizzle the mixture with the orange juice and sprinkle with the cinnamon. Add the butter, stir, and cover.

3 Bake just until the apples are tender, 20 to 30 minutes.

Makes 4 servings

"Granny used to call this one 'chocolate gravy' because she often poured it over homemade biscuits. One summer when we were kids, my city cousins came to visit, and they experienced Granny's chocolate gravy for the first time. I think it was a religious experience for them because they still talk about it more than thirty years later. A southern recipe, this sauce is great served over homemade biscuits or apple dumplings. You can also use it over ice cream or any dessert that needs a basic homemade topping."

2 cups sugar

6 tablespoons flour

6 teaspoons unsweetened cocoa powder

6 cups milk

Butter (optional)

1 Combine the sugar, flour, and cocoa in a medium saucepan off the heat. Stir in the milk.

2 Cook and stir over medium heat until the sauce thickens.

3 Add some butter for extra richness, if desired.

Makes 6 cups

J.R.'S GRANNY'S "CHOCOLATE GRAVY"

AWN MICHAELS   JIM CORNETTE   HARDY BOYZ   UNDERTAKER   TRISH STRATUS   BIG SHOW   TRIP
YZ   CHRIS BENOIT   DEAN MALENKO   RIKISHI   KAIENTAI   DROZ   D'LO BROWN   JERRY "THE KING"
LBOWSKI   THE KAT   STEVE BLACKMAN   STEVE REGAL   HARVEY WHIPPLEMAN   VINCE MCMAHON
LY GUNN   ROAD DOGG   BULLDOG   AL SNOW   HILLBILLY JIM   HEADBANGERS   MICHAEL COLE
INCE ALBERT   GERALD BRISCO   KURT ANGLE   THE GODFATHER   X-PAC   CRASH HOLLY   VISCERA   PE
TA MANKIND   EDGE   GANGREL   CHYNA   SCOTTY TOO HOTTY   STEPHANIE MCMAHON-HELMSLEY
M CORNETTE   HARDY BOYZ   UNDERTAKER   TRISH STRATUS   BIG SHOW   TRIPLE H   BRADSHAW   PA
AN MALENKO   RIKISHI   KAIENTAI   DROZ   D'LO BROWN   JERRY "THE KING" LAWLER   MEAN STRE
EVE BLACKMAN   STEVE REGAL   HARVEY WHIPPLEMAN   VINCE MCMAHON   IVORY   TORI   PAUL BEA
LLDOG   AL SNOW   HILLBILLY JIM   HEADBANGERS   MICHAEL COLE   CHYNA   TEST   TERRI   ACOLY
ISCO   KURT ANGLE   THE GODFATHER   X-PAC   CRASH HOLLY   VISCERA   PERRY SATURN   CHRIS JE
NGREL   CHYNA   SCOTTY TOO HOTTY   STEPHANIE MCMAHON-HELMSLEY   J.R.   ESSA RIOS   BULL B
YZ   UNDERTAKER   TRISH STRATUS   BIG SHOW   TRIPLE H   BRADSHAW   PAT PATTERSON   BIG BOSS
IENTAI   DROZ   D'LO BROWN   JERRY "THE KING" LAWLER   MEAN STREET POSSE   SHANE MCMAH
GAL   HARVEY WHIPPLEMAN   VINCE MCMAHON   IVORY   TORI   PAUL BEARER   FAAROOQ   MICHAE
LLBILLY JIM   HEADBANGERS   MICHAEL COLE   CHYNA   TEST   TERRI   ACOLYTES   TAZZ   STEVEN RICH
DFATHER   X-PAC   CRASH HOLLY   VISCERA   PERRY SATURN   CHRIS JERICHO   BOB BACKLUND   DEB
O HOTTY   STEPHANIE MCMAHON-HELMSLEY   J.R.   ESSA RIOS   BULL BUCHANAN   MIDEON   HOWAR
RATUS   BIG SHOW   TRIPLE H   BRADSHAW   PAT PATTERSON   BIG BOSS MAN   THE BROOKLYN
OWN   JERRY "THE KING" LAWLER   MEAN STREET POSSE   SHANE MCMAHON
HIPPLEMAN   VINCE MCMAHON   IVORY   TORI   PAUL

VICTORY CELEBRAT

ADBANGERS   MICHAEL COLE   CHYNA   TEST   TERRI   ACOLYTES   TAZZ   STEVEN RICHARDS   KANE
C   CRASH HOLLY   VISCERA   PERRY SATURN   CHRIS JERICHO   BOB BACKLUND   DEBRA   FABULOUS
EPHANIE MCMAHON-HELMSLEY   J.R.   ESSA RIOS   BULL BUCHANAN   MIDEON   HOWARD FINKEL
G SHOW   TRIPLE H   BRADSHAW   PAT PATTERSON   BIG BOSS MAN   THE BROOKLYN BRAWLER   HARD
HE KING" LAWLER   MEAN STREET POSSE   SHANE MCMAHON   CHRISTIAN   JACQUELINE   EDDIE GU
CMAHON   IVORY   TORI   PAUL BEARER   FAAROOQ   MICHAEL HAYES   TOO COOL   GRAND MASTER SEX
LE   CHYNA   TEST   TERRI   ACOLYTES   TAZZ   STEVEN RICHARDS   KANE   CLASSY FREDDY BLASSI
SCERA   PERRY SATURN   CHRIS JERICHO   BOB BACKLUND   DEBRA   FABULOUS MOOLAH   MAE YOUNG
LMSLEY   J.R.   ESSA RIOS   BULL BUCHANAN   MIDEON   HOWARD FINKEL   THE ROCK   STONE COLD
ADSHAW   PAT PATTERSON   BIG BOSS MAN   THE BROOKLYN BRAWLER   HARDCORE HOLLY   DUDLEY
EAN STREET POSSE   SHANE MCMAHON   CHRISTIAN   JACQUELINE   EDDIE GUERRERO   THE BIG VALB
UL BEARER   FAAROOQ   MICHAEL HAYES   TOO COOL   GRAND MASTER SEXAY   DUDLEY BOYZ   BILLY GU
OLYTES   TAZZ   STEVEN RICHARDS   KANE   CLASSY FREDDY BLASSIE   MARK HENRY   PRINCE ALBER
RICHO   BOB BACKLUND   DEBRA   FABULOUS MOOLAH   MAE YOUNG   SGT. SLAUGHTER   LITA   MANKIN
CHANAN   MIDEON   HOWARD FINKEL   THE ROCK   STONE COLD   SHAWN MICHAELS   JIM CORNETT
SS MAN   THE BROOKLYN BRAWLER   HARDCORE HOLLY   DUDLEY BOYZ   CHRIS BENOIT   DEAN MAL
CMAHON   CHRISTIAN   JACQUELINE   EDDIE GUERRERO   THE BIG VALBOWSKI   THE KAT   STEVE BLA
CHAEL HAYES   TOO COOL   GRAND MASTER SEXAY   DUDLEY BOYZ   BILLY GUNN   ROAD DOGG   BU
EVEN RICHARDS   KANE   CLASSY FREDDY BLASSIE   MARK HENRY   PRINCE ALBERT   GERALD BRIS

ON: Beverages

SGT. SLAUGHTER'S REVEILLE COFFEE

"**Sarge received so much heat** when his TV persona 'turned his back on his country' that the Minnesota native actually received death threats! That's probably taking the sport just a little too seriously, folks. Sarge is serious about coffee, and he often serves this specialty to houseguests."

Ground coffee to taste

Ground cinnamon to taste

Sugar to taste

Milk, cream, or flavored coffee creamer to taste

1 Rise and shine, sleepyheads! *At-ten-hut!*

2 Okay, at ease and listen up. When preparing your morning coffee, just add ground cinnamon to the top of the coffee grounds before you start your percolator, coffeemaker, or coffee brewer. Add 1 teaspoon ground cinnamon for every 2 cups of coffee you're making.

3 Have I made myself clear? I can't hear you! Good, then carry on!

4 Add sugar, milk, cream, or flavored coffee creamer, to your liking.

5 Any questions? Good, then enjoy, and that's an order! You're dismissed!

"I use a coffee brewer (such as Mr. Coffee) with a programmable clock, so my Reveille coffee is ready for me at **0500**. The smell of the coffee brewing acts as my alarm clock, and the coffee is ready and waiting for me before I head over to the barracks and get my 'privates' moving!"

FABULOUS MOOLAH AND MAE YOUNG'S AFTER-DINNER SPECIALTY COFFEES

"These two ladies are both on the north side of seventy and still kickin'! Both wrestle a few times a year—extraordinary! Superstars in a predominately male rasslin' world for more than half a century, Moolah and Mae are no strangers to a good cigar and a strong beverage—in moderation, of course. Be careful, but do proceed. Our favorite ladies have had many years to perfect these beverages, so they can't be wrong."

Irish Coffee Stir 1 to 2 tablespoons Irish whiskey and 1 to 2 teaspoons sugar together in the bottom of a coffee cup. Pour in strong coffee, stir, and top with whipped cream.

Kahlúa Coffee Stir 1 to 2 tablespoons Kahlúa into a cup of coffee. Top with whipped cream and garnish with grated orange zest.

Amaretto Coffee Stir 1 to 2 tablespoons amaretto liqueur into a cup of coffee. Top with light whipped cream, and garnish with slivered almonds.

CRASH HOLLY'S JELL-O SHOOTERS

"**The key word here** is *moderation.* This is a refreshing XFL tailgate party beverage that should be consumed responsibly, and by adults only. Our boy Elroy would probably do well to avoid this delectable but dangerous beverage."

1 (6-ounce) box lime Jell-O
Vodka
12 (1-ounce) paper cups

1 Follow the directions on the box of Jell-O, but replace the cold water with the vodka instead.

2 Pour the liquid into the cups and refrigerate for 2 hours.

Makes 12 shooters

Enjoy at tailgate parties or as an hors d'oeuvre. Limit two per person or BEWARE!!!!!

TORI'S
BANANA-ORANGE SMOOTHIE

"No one eats and drinks healthier than Tori, who downs several of these babies every week. By the looks of her, they work."

2 (8-ounce) containers low-fat strawberry, orange, or plain yogurt

2 bananas, peeled and cut into pieces

2 seedless oranges, peeled, white pith removed, cut into segments

16 frozen dark cherries (optional)

12 frozen strawberries

1 Combine 1 container of yogurt, 1 banana, 1 orange, 8 cherries, and 6 strawberries in a blender.

2 Blend on medium speed until smooth.

3 Divide between 2 glasses.

4 Repeat with the remaining ingredients.

Makes 4 servings

ACKNOWLEDGMENTS

The following people are to be thanked for their tremendous help in putting this book together:

Recipes:
Jim Ross
Jan Ross
Kevin Kelly
Doria Foote
All the World Wrestling Federation personalities

World Wrestling Federation editor:
Dennis Brent

Front and back jacket photo shoot (coordination and production):
Jim Ross
Stone Cold Steve Austin
The Rock
Debra
Mike (not Mick!) Foley
Debbie DeGeralomo
Debbie Bonnanzio
Dave Barry
Lynn Brent
Dennis Brent
Nicole Dorazio
Kit Nobel, photographer
Rachel Campbell, food stylist
Jill Clark, makeup
John Thorme, security, Greenwich Police Department
Special thanks to Jan Ross for getting the jacket project on track, being instrumental in making it happen, and allowing us to use her kitchen.

WWF photographs:
Noelle Soper (World Wrestling Federation photo editor)
Tom Buchanan (World Wrestling Federation senior photographer)
Rich Freda (World Wrestling Federation photographer)

We would also like to thank Scott Amann and Derek Phillips at the World Wrestling Federation for all of their hard work, as well as Tia Maggini, our editor at ReganBooks.

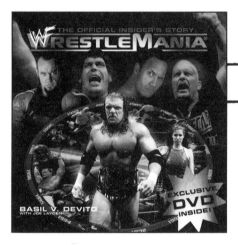

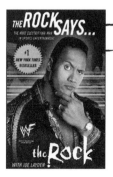